C0-BOR-484

FIELD GUIDE TO

MICROSOFT
POWERPOINT 4

Stephen L. Nelson

Microsoft
P R E S S
®

The Field Guide to Microsoft PowerPoint is divided into four sections. These sections are designed to help you find the information you need quickly.

1 ENVIRONMENT

Terms and ideas you'll want to know to get the most out of PowerPoint. All the basic parts of PowerPoint are shown and explained. The emphasis here is on quick answers, but most topics are cross-referenced so that you can find out more if you want to.

Diagrams of key windows components, with quick definitions, cross-referenced to more complete information.

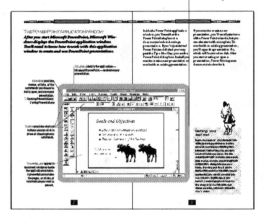

Tipmeister

Watch for me as you use this Field Guide. I'll point out helpful hints and let you know what to watch for.

11 POWERPOINT A to Z

An alphabetic list of commands, tasks, terms, and procedures.

Definitions of key concepts and terms, and examples showing you why you should know them.

Quick identification of icons and groups.

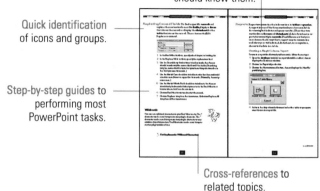

Step-by-step guides to performing most PowerPoint tasks.

Cross-references to related topics.

135 TROUBLESHOOTING

A guide to common problems—how to avoid them and what to do when they occur.

151 QUICK REFERENCE

Useful indexes, including a full list of menu commands, shortcut keys, and more.

167 INDEX

A complete reference to all elements of the Field Guide.

INTRODUCTION

In the field and on expedition, you need practical solutions. Fast. This Field Guide provides just these sorts of lightning quick answers. But take two minutes and read the Introduction. It explains how this unusual little book works.

WHAT IS A FIELD GUIDE?

Sometime during grade school, my parents gave me a field guide to North American birds. With its visual approach, its maps, and its numerous illustrations, that guide delivered hours of enjoyment. The book also helped me better understand and more fully appreciate the birds in my neighborhood. And the small book fit neatly in a child's rucksack. But I'm getting off the track.

This book works in the same way as that field guide. It organizes information visually with numerous illustrations. And it does this in a way that helps you more easily understand and, yes, even enjoy working with Microsoft PowerPoint. For new users, the Field Guide provides a visual path to the essential information necessary to start using Microsoft PowerPoint. But the Field Guide isn't only for beginners. For experienced users, it provides concise, easy-to-find descriptions of Microsoft PowerPoint tasks, terms, and techniques.

HOW TO USE THIS BOOK

Let me explain how to find the information you need. You'll usually want to begin with the first section, Environment, which is really a visual index. You find the picture that shows what you want to do or the task you have a question about. If you want to know how to add a text to a slide, for example, you flip to pp. 4–5, which show a presentation outline and a slide with text.

Next you read the captions that describe the parts of the picture—or key elements of Microsoft PowerPoint. Say, for example, that you're new to the business of creating presentations and want to become familiar with PowerPoint terms such as **views** and **slides.** The window on pp. 4–5 includes captions that describe presentation views and slides. These key elements appear in **boldface** type to make them stand out.

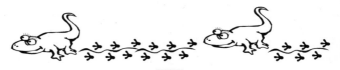

You'll notice that some captions are followed by a little paw print and additional **boldface** terms. These refer to entries in the second section, PowerPoint A to Z, and provide more information related to the caption's contents. (The paw print shows you how to track down the information you need. Get it?)

PowerPoint A to Z is a dictionary of more than 100 entries that define terms and describe tasks. (After you've worked with Microsoft PowerPoint a bit or if you're already an experienced user, you'll often be able to turn directly to this section.) So, if you have just read the caption that says Microsoft Excel charts can be added to a presentation slide as **OLE objects,** you can flip to the OLE Objects entry in PowerPoint A to Z.

Any time an entry in PowerPoint A to Z appears as a term within an entry, I'll **boldface** it the first time it appears in the entry. For example, as part of describing what an **Autolayout** is, I tell you that it includes **placeholders.** In this case, the word placeholder will appear in bold letters—alerting you to the presence of a Placeholder entry. If you don't understand the term or want to do a bit of brushing up, you can flip to the entry for more information.

The third section, Troubleshooting, describes problems that new or casual users of Microsoft PowerPoint often encounter. Following each problem description, I list one or more solutions you can employ to fix the problem.

The Quick Reference describes the menu commands and toolbar tools that appear on the PowerPoint application window and the Graph application window. (Graph is a supplementary application that comes with PowerPoint. You can use it to add charts to slides.) If you want to know what a specific command does, turn to the Quick Reference. Don't forget about the Index either. You can look there to find all references in this book to any single topic.

CONVENTIONS USED HERE

I have developed some conventions to make using this book easier for you. Rather than use wordy phrases, such as "Activate the File menu and then choose the Print command," to describe how you choose a command, I'm just going to say, "Choose the File Print command."

When some technique requires you to click a toolbar button, I'm going to tell you to select the tool. (I'll show a picture of the tool in the margin, so you won't have any trouble identifying it.)

ENVIRONMENT

Need to get the lay of the land quickly? Then the Environment is the place to start. It defines the key terms you'll need to know and the core ideas you should understand as you begin exploring Microsoft PowerPoint.

THE POWERPOINT APPLICATION WINDOW

After you start Microsoft PowerPoint, Microsoft Windows displays the PowerPoint application window. You'll need to know how to work with this application window to create and use PowerPoint presentations.

Title bars identify the **application**—Microsoft PowerPoint—and name your **presentation**.

Menu bar provides menus, or lists, of the commands you choose to build, open, and save your presentation.
❖ **Opening Presentations; Saving Presentations**

Toolbar provides shortcut buttons you can click in place of choosing menu commands.

Presentations appear in **document windows** inside the **application window**. A presentation includes the pages, or **slides,** of information you want to present.

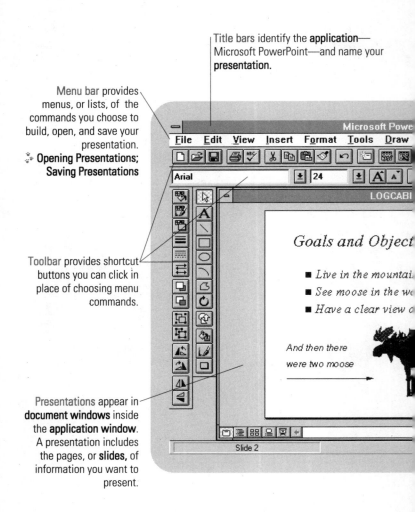

Inside the PowerPoint **application window,** you'll see either the PowerPoint dialog box or a **document window** showing a **presentation.** If you've just started PowerPoint and clicked your way past the **Tip of the Day,** you see the PowerPoint dialog box. It asks if you want to create a new presentation or work with an existing presentation.

If you want to create a new presentation, you'll usually start one of the PowerPoint **wizards,** but you can also start with a **template.** To work with an existing presentation, you'll open the presentation **file,** which will be stored on disk. After you start creating or open a presentation, PowerPoint opens a document window for it.

Getting your feet wet

Learn the basics of the Microsoft Windows operating environment before you start learning and working with Microsoft PowerPoint. No, you don't need to become an expert. But you should know how to choose commands from menus. And you should know how to work with dialog box elements: boxes, buttons, and lists. If you've worked with another Windows-based application, you almost certainly possess this core knowledge. If you haven't, I encourage you to read the first chapter of the Windows user documentation, *Microsoft Windows User's Guide.*

CREATING A PRESENTATION

To create a presentation, your first step will usually be to start a wizard either to help you organize a presentation's information or to design its appearance.

AutoContent Wizard creates a preliminary **outline** for your presentation based on its purpose and displays this outline in a document window called Outline **view,** as shown here. To create the presentation text, you edit the suggested **slide titles** and slide text.
❖ **Text Boxes; Text Objects**

Views are different ways of looking at the information in a presentation. Outline view shows the **slide titles** and slide text. Slide view shows the actual way a slide looks.
❖ **Notes Pages; Slide Show; Slide Sorter**

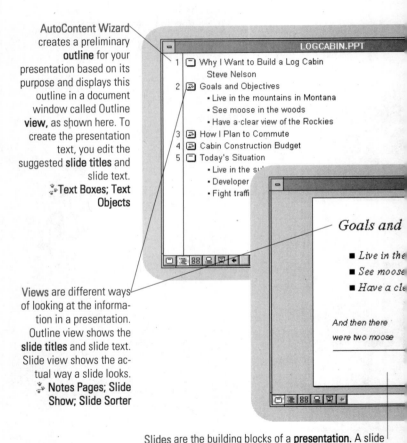

Slides are the building blocks of a **presentation.** A slide can include text, as shown here. It can also include **Graph** charts, **clip art, tables, pictures,** and even objects created by other applications.
❖ **Object Linking and Embedding**

After you start PowerPoint, it displays the PowerPoint dialog box that asks, among other questions, if you want to start the **AutoContent Wizard** to help you organize the presentation's information and help with the overall appearance or if you want to work with an existing presentation. You'll find it valuable—especially when you're a new or infrequent PowerPoint user—to use the AutoContent Wizard because it lets you name the slides, or pages, in a presentation and provide slide text. To use a PowerPoint **wizard,** you answer the questions posed in a series of dialog boxes.

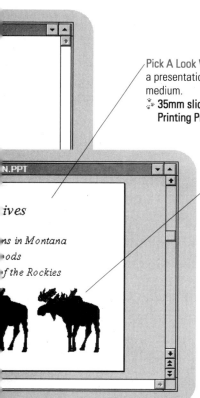

ives

ns in Montana
ods
f the Rockies

Pick A Look Wizard helps you modify the appearance of a presentation so that it's compatible with the output medium.
✢ 35mm slides; Color Scheme; Pick A Look Wizard; Printing Presentations

Visual elements of a slide get inserted as objects. PowerPoint lets you add charts, **clip art** (shown here), and **organization charts** to **slides.** You can also use **object linking and embedding** to add **OLE objects** such as **Microsoft Word** tables or **Microsoft Excel** worksheets.
✢ Drawing

Templates provide a shortcut for experienced users

If you know what you want to say and how you want your presentation to look, you might not want to use either of PowerPoint's wizards. You might instead want to use a template.

SHARING INFORMATION

Although PowerPoint lets you create all the raw data needed for a presentation, you'll often create the pieces of a presentation elsewhere.

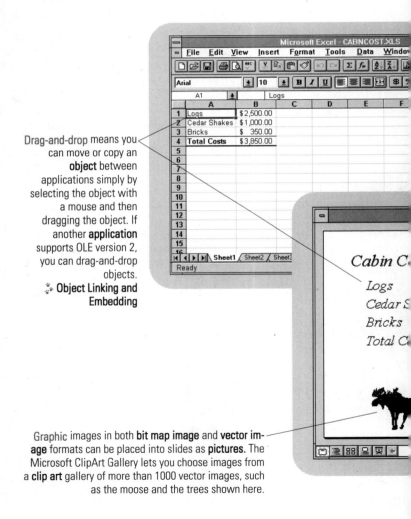

Drag-and-drop means you can move or copy an **object** between applications simply by selecting the object with a mouse and then dragging the object. If another **application** supports OLE version 2, you can drag-and-drop objects.
❖ **Object Linking and Embedding**

Graphic images in both **bit map image** and **vector image** formats can be placed into slides as **pictures**. The Microsoft ClipArt Gallery lets you choose images from a **clip art** gallery of more than 1000 vector images, such as the moose and the trees shown here.

You might, for example, have a clip art image you want to use in a presentation. And you might have documents or chunks of documents you've created in other applications that you want to use in a presentation: tables from a word processor, for example, or worksheets or charts from a spreadsheet.

Supplementary applications that come with PowerPoint let you add visual elements such as clip art, **organization charts,** and **WordArt** to your **slides.**

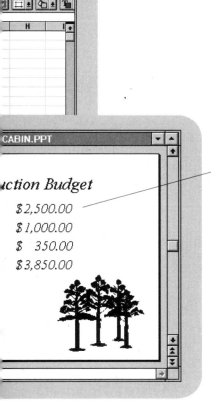

In-place editing is available for objects created by **applications** supporting OLE version 2. It means you can make changes to embedded objects without having to leave PowerPoint and start the other application.

❖ Object Linking and Embedding

PRESENTATION OUTPUT

PowerPoint lets you show the information in a presentation in a variety of ways.

Print presentations to create **speaker's notes,** transparencies, or audience handout pages. You aren't limited to showing a presentation in black and white or on paper: You can use on-screen projections, color output, and even color transparencies if your printer allows.

❖ Handouts; Printing
   Presentations

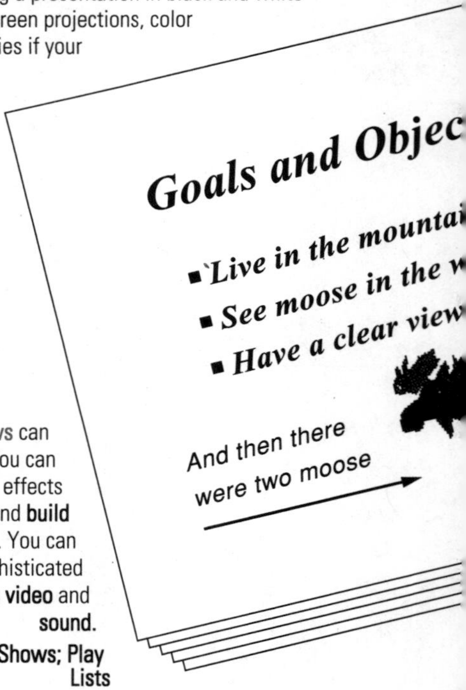

Electronic slide shows can use special effects. You can use simple special effects such as **transitions** and **build slides,** for example. You can also use more sophisticated effects such as **video** and **sound.**

❖ Looping Slide Shows; Play
   Lists

Goals and Objec

■ `Live in the mountai
■ See moose in the v
■ Have a clear view

And then there
were two moose →

You can show a presentation electronically on a computer, such as in a series of full-screen **slide shows.** You can print audience **handouts** in black and white or color. And you can also output presentations to special media such as **35mm slides.**

35mm slides can be created with a film recorder or the help of a service bureau.

PowerPoint Viewer, a separate **application** that comes with PowerPoint, lets you distribute PowerPoint presentations even to people who don't own PowerPoint, and lets you show presentations on computers that don't have PowerPoint installed.

᠅ **Viewer**

For quick 35mm slides

PowerPoint comes with GraphicsLink, a telecommunications program. GraphicsLink lets you electronically transmit 35mm slide files to Genigraphics for quick turnaround.

9

POWERPOINT A TO Z

Maybe it's not a jungle out there. But you'll still want to keep a survival kit close at hand. PowerPoint A to Z, which starts on the next page, is just such a survival kit. It lists in alphabetic order the tools, terms, and techniques you'll need to know.

35mm Slides You can create 35mm slides for a PowerPoint **presentation.** (Be sure that you first adjust your **slide setup** so that PowerPoint knows you want the 35mm slide size.)

If you have a film recorder installed on your personal computer, you can simply *print* to the film recorder. The film recorder will photograph your slides. You can then send the undeveloped film to a film developer who will turn your undeveloped film into 35mm slides. (I have no idea how they do this last part. My high school photography class was full when I got to the registration desk.)

If you don't have a film recorder, you can create a print **file** for a film recorder, send the print file to someone who has a film recorder (such as a service bureau), and then have them *print* to a film recorder and develop the film. If you have a modem, you can probably send the file electronically. PowerPoint comes with a Genigraphics driver that you'll need to install and activate before printing.

Printing to a film recorder

Of course, you don't actually print to a film recorder. You send it digital copies of your slides, which it displays and photographs. I've referred to this processing as printing to the film recorder only because you use the File Print command.

❖ Printing Presentations

Active and Inactive Windows The active **document window** is the one you see in front of any other document windows in the **application window.** Any commands you choose affect the **document** in the active document window.

The active application window—such as the PowerPoint application window—is the one that appears in front of any other application window on your screen. (Cleverly, this is called the foreground. The inactive application windows, if there are any, appear in the background.)

Activating Document Windows

You can activate a different document window by clicking the window, by pressing Ctrl+F6, or by choosing the Window menu command that names the window. PowerPoint presentations are displayed in document windows.

Activating Application Windows

You can activate a different application window by clicking the window or by choosing the Switch To command from the Control menu.

Active Presentation

The active **presentation** is the one you can see in front of any other presentations in the PowerPoint **application window**. It's also the presentation upon which selected commands act.

If you're familiar with the whole notion of Windows documents, you might be interested in knowing that—at least from Windows' point of view—PowerPoint presentations are documents and are displayed in document windows.

Changing the active presentation

You can flip-flop between open presentations—if you have more than one open—by choosing one of the numbered menu commands from the Window menu. Each numbered command names an open **document window.** You can also press Ctrl+F6 to move to the next document window.

Alignment You can change the alignment of the text within a **text object** using the Format Alignment submenu commands: Left, Center, Right, and Justify. Or you can change the alignment of text with the Formatting toolbar alignment tools: Left and Center.

Annotating Slides You can add notes and other scribbles to slides during a slide show. Select the Freehand tool that appears in the lower right of the screen during slide shows. Then drag the mouse to write or make the marks you want. You'll want to practice your mouse-dragging a bit before you try this in front of other people. It's harder than it looks.

This scribble is a freehand annotation. PowerPoint erases the annotation when you press E or move to another slide.

ANSI Characters The ANSI character set includes all the ASCII characters your keyboard shows plus the special characters your keyboard doesn't show, such as the Japanese yen symbol, ¥, or the British pound symbol, £. Even though these special characters don't appear on your keyboard, you can still use them in most Windows-based applications—including PowerPoint. You can, for example, enter ANSI characters into **text boxes**.

A

Adding ANSI Characters

To enter an ANSI character, position the **insertion point** in the **text object** where you want the character, hold down Alt, and then, using the numeric keypad, enter the ANSI code for that character. For example, the ANSI character code for the Japanese yen symbol is 0165. To enter a yen symbol into a document, hold down Alt and type *0165* using the numeric keypad. Be sure to include the zero. (Refer to the Windows user documentation for a list of ANSI character codes.)

Removing ANSI Characters

To delete an ANSI character, select it and press Del, or backspace over the character.

⁘ **Character Map**

Apple Macintosh

It's amazingly easily to move a PowerPoint **presentation** you create on an IBM compatible personal computer running Windows to an Apple Macintosh personal computer. Amazingly easy. All you do is save your presentation in the usual way—except to a floppy disk.

Then—and I'll just briefly overview the mechanics here because this book isn't about the Apple Macintosh—you start the Apple File Exchange utility, which comes with Macintosh, and copy the presentation **file** from your floppy disk to your Macintosh's hard disk.

Sure. You may not think you want to do this right now. But just wait. Sooner or later, you'll want to share a PowerPoint presentation you've created with somebody who uses an Apple Macintosh. Then you'll be glad I've broached the subject.

Technical tidbits about Apple File Exchange

To use Apple File Exchange, by the way, you (or the Mac user) will probably need to install it. Apple doesn't install it automatically. This Macintosh you're moving your presentation to must have a SuperDrive, which is a floppy drive capable of reading and writing both IBM compatible and Apple Macintosh floppy disks. For more information about how to install and use Apple File Exchange, refer to the Macintosh Reference manual. Enough said, right?

Application Applications are the programs you buy down at the software store or through the mail to do work—work such as word processing, accounting, or even presentation creating. PowerPoint, for example, is an application.

About PowerPoint's supplementary applications

PowerPoint isn't the only application that comes in the PowerPoint box. You also get four additional Microsoft applications: Graph, Organization Chart, WordArt, and Viewer. You can use the first three of these applications and Windows' Object Linking and Embedding to add graphs, organizational charts, and WordArt objects to the slides or pages of a PowerPoint presentation.

    Exiting PowerPoint; Starting PowerPoint

Application Window The application window is the rectangle in which an **application** such as PowerPoint, **Microsoft Excel,** or **Microsoft Word** displays its menu bar, **toolbars,** and any open **document windows.**

Audience Handout Pages ⸪ **Handouts**

AutoContent Wizard The AutoContent Wizard helps you organize your **presentation** by providing what amounts to a boilerplate structure. I know this sounds crazy. How can the folks at Microsoft know the form your, say, sales presentation should take? Well, they don't know all the specifics, of course. But they have developed some good ideas as to how one goes about organizing different types of presentations. You'll still need to flesh out the details. But the AutoContent Wizard will provide a framework for you to begin building.

Starting the AutoContent Wizard

When you start PowerPoint, it displays the PowerPoint dialog box. One of the option buttons on the dialog box is the AutoContent Wizard. If you select this option button and choose OK, PowerPoint starts the AutoContent Wizard.

 If you want to start a new presentation and organize it with the AutoContent Wizard when you are already in PowerPoint, you can choose the File New command or select the New tool. Doing either also causes PowerPoint to display the PowerPoint dialog box. Again, you select the AutoContent Wizard option and choose OK to start the wizard.

Once you've started the AutoContent Wizard, PowerPoint displays the first AutoContent Wizard dialog box.

Running the AutoContent Wizard

To run the AutoContent Wizard, follow these steps:

1 Start the AutoContent Wizard. PowerPoint displays the first AutoContent Wizard dialog box.

2 Select Next. The wizard asks for some information it will put on the **Slide Master** and, therefore, use in each of the **slides** in your presentation.

3 Fill in the text boxes on the second AutoContent Wizard dialog box. The presentation title should go into the first box. PowerPoint automatically plugs in your name and your company name, by the way, as the presenter and presenting company. The presenter's name is a subtitle.

continues

AutoContent Wizard *(continued)*

4 Select Next. The wizard asks about the type of presentation you're making. You select the option button that most closely describes your presentation.

5 Select Next. The wizard displays the checkered flag, indicating you're done.

6 Select Finish. The wizard displays a rough **outline** for your presentation using Outline **view.** You'll probably want to work with this outline to finish organizing your presentation and to enter any of the textual information—such as bulleted lists—you want to include.

 Bullets

AutoLayouts
PowerPoint offers 21 AutoLayouts, or blueprints, for the **slides** in a **presentation.** The neat thing about AutoLayouts is that they provide **placeholders** you can use to easily create your slides.

Choosing an AutoLayout

When you add a slide to a presentation—such as by using the Insert New Slide tool or the Insert New Slide command—and you're looking at the presentation in Slide **view,** you can choose one of these layouts from the New Slide dialog box.

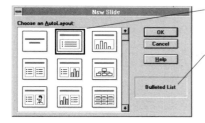

To select an AutoLayout for the new slide, click it. Then choose OK.

PowerPoint names the selected AutoLayout.

Reviewing the Available AutoLayouts
The table below names and describes each of the 21 AutoLayouts.

Sketch	Description
	Title Slide usually names your presentation. It's typically the first slide displayed.
	Bulleted List provides a ready-to-be filled bulleted list.
	Graph provides a slide with a graph **placeholder.** Double-click the graph placeholder to start Graph and use it to add a graph.
	2 Column Text provides a slide with two ready-to-be-filled **text boxes** for entering a couple of textual blurbs. Click a text box and bang away at your keyboard to add text.

continues

AutoLayouts *(continued)*

Sketch	Description
	Text & Graph provides a slide with a ready-to-be-filled text box and a graph placeholder. Click on a text box and then add text. Double-click the graph placeholder to start Graph and use it to add a graph.
	Org Chart provides a slide with an organization chart placeholder. Double-click the organization chart placeholder to start Organization Chart and add an organization chart.
	Text & Clip Art provides a slide with a ready-to-be-filled text box and a clip art placeholder. Add text to the text box in the usual way: Click and type. Double-click the clip art placeholder to start ClipArt Gallery and use it to add clip art.
	Graph & Text AutoLayout is identical to Text & Graph AutoLayout except that the text box and graph placeholders are flip-flopped.
	Table provides a slide with a Microsoft Word table placeholder. Double-click the table placeholder to get the Insert Word Table dialog box and add a table.
	Clip Art & Text AutoLayout is identical to the Text & Clip Art AutoLayout except that the text box and clip art placeholders are flip-flopped.
	Text & Object provides a slide with a ready-to-be-filled text box and an object placeholder. Add text to the text box in the usual way. Double-click the object placeholder to insert an existing or a new object—such as a chunk of WordArt.
	Object provides a slide with an object placeholder. Double-click the object placeholder to insert an existing or a new object.
	Text & 2 Objects AutoLayout is similar to the Text & Object AutoLayout. With this layout, however, you've got two object placeholders instead of only one.

Sketch	Description
	Object & Text AutoLayout is identical to the Text & Object AutoLayout except that the text box and object placeholders are flip-flopped.
	Object over Text AutoLayout is similar to the Object & Text AutoLayout except that the text box and object placeholder positions differ.
	2 Objects & Text AutoLayout is identical to the Text & 2 Objects AutoLayout except that the text box and two object placeholders are flip-flopped.
	2 Objects over Text AutoLayout is similar to the Text & 2 Objects AutoLayout except that the text box and object placeholder positions differ.
	Text over Object AutoLayout is identical to the Object over Text AutoLayout except that the text box and object placeholders are flip-flopped.
	4 Objects provides a slide with four object placeholders. Double-click an object placeholder to add an object.
	Title Only provides a slide with only a title placeholder. But you probably guessed as much from the AutoLayout name.
	Blank provides an empty slide with no placeholders. Blank slides are a good way to end a presentation. You can also add text, graphs, organization charts, and objects to the slide by using Insert menu commands.

Embedding and Linking Existing Objects; Embedding New Objects

Backgrounds The background you specify for the **Slide Master** determines the background color and any background artwork for all the **slides** in your **presentation.** If you want to change the slide background, modify the Slide Master.

    Color Schemes

Bit Map Images A bit map is simply a pattern of colored dots. On your screen, each colored dot is created as a pixel of light and is described by one or more bits (binary digits). This sounds like a bunch of gobbledygook, but if the pattern arranges the colored dots in the right way, you get a picture.

As a point of historical reference, I'll also mention that probably the best known bit maps were those created in the late 19th century by the French impressionist painter Seurat. In this case, however, the colored dots were created by brushstrokes of paint on canvas rather than by pixels of light. And you thought this book was just about computers.

You can create bit map images with a variety of **applications,** such as the Windows Paintbrush accessory. You can insert bit map images in a **presentation** using the Insert Picture command. One problem with bit map images, however, is that they aren't very easy to edit. To edit a bit map image, you need to recolor the individual pixels of colors. (In comparison, the **vector image** produced by a drawing program consists of drawing **objects** that can be much more easily edited.)

Bold Characters You can bold characters by selecting them and then either pressing Ctrl+B or selecting the Bold tool. **B** You can also use the Format Font command.

    Fonts

Branching You can embed **presentations** as **drill-down documents,** or **objects,** in other presentations. If a person viewing a presentation double-clicks one of these objects, he or she sees the other presentation. This ability to move from one presentation to another is called branching.

> **Embedding and Linking Existing Objects; Embedding New Objects; Object Linking and Embedding**

Build Slides When you have a **slide** with a bulleted list, you can choose to display the bullet points one at a time rather than all at once. In PowerPoint, slides that work this way are called build slides.

To create a build slide, follow these steps:

1 Display the Slide Sorter view—such as by choosing the View Slide Sorter command.

2 Select the slides that have bulleted lists that you want to turn into build slides.

3 Choose the Tools Build command. Or select the Build tool. PowerPoint displays the Build dialog box.

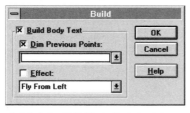

4 Mark the Build Body Text check box.

5 Mark the Dim Previous Points check box, and select a color from its drop-down list box if you want previously displayed bullet points displayed in a different color so that the most recently displayed bullet point stands out.

6 Mark the Effect check box, and select the build effect from its drop-down list.

7 Choose OK.

Bullets   The **paragraphs** in a **text object** are by default treated as bullet points. What this really means, just in case you care, is that each chunk of text you enter is formatted with a hanging indent and a bullet symbol.

Removing the Bullets

You can remove the bullets from a bulleted list by selecting the Bullet On/Off tool. Even when you remove the bullets from the selected paragraph or paragraphs, the paragraph will be formatted with a hanging indent.

Replacing the Bullets

If you want to use another bullet symbol, follow these steps:

1   Select the bullet point, the set of bullet points, or the text object with the bullets you want to change.

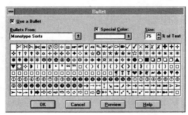

2   Choose the Format Bullet command. PowerPoint displays the Bullet dialog box.

3   Use the Bullets From list box to specify from which font you want to use a bullet symbol. To add a skull and crossbones character to a document, for example, you would specify Wingdings. After you specify the font set, PowerPoint displays a grid of the characters.

4   Select the character by clicking the mouse. When you select a character, PowerPoint magnifies it.

5   Use the Special Color check box and drop-down list box to specify the bullet character's color. (The Special Color options are available only in Slide view.)

6   Use the Size box to specify the size of the bullet as a percentage of the text size.

7   Choose OK to replace the selected text's bullets.

Case

You can change the case—uppercase *vs.* lowercase—of the selected text by using the Format Change Case command. After you choose the command, PowerPoint displays a dialog box that provides option buttons corresponding to your choices.

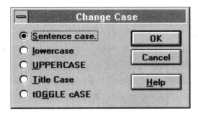

Character Map

The Character Map **application** lets you easily add characters that don't appear on your keyboard to **documents** such as PowerPoint **presentations.** For example, if you want to add one of the following Wingdings characters, or symbols, to a document, the easiest and only practical way is to use Character Map.

Starting Character Map

Start Character Map by displaying the Accessories group and then double-clicking the Character Map program item.

continues

Character Map *(continued)*

Using Character Map

To use Character Map, follow these steps:

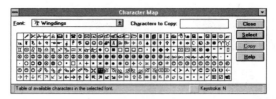

1 Activate the Font drop-down list box, and select the font with the character you want. (If you want to enlarge the symbol after you add it, you'll find that scalable fonts such as **TrueType** or PostScript fonts work best.)

2 Find the character you want. If you can't see the character very well—and I never can—click the character box and hold down the mouse button. Character Map displays a pop-up box showing an enlarged version of the character.

3 Choose the Select command button. Character Map places the selected character in the Characters to Copy text box.

4 Optionally, repeat steps 2 and 3 to add more characters to the Characters to Copy text box.

5 Choose the Copy command button. (Doing so copies the selected characters to the **Clipboard**.)

6 Switch to the application containing the document into which you want to place the special characters—say, PowerPoint—position the **insertion point,** and then choose Edit Paste.

7 Format the newly inserted characters so that they use the same font you selected in step 1.

 Fonts

Character Spacing Character spacing, also known as kerning, refers to the way characters are spaced in a word. PowerPoint itself doesn't let you control character spacing. You can, however, control character spacing for the text used in **WordArt** objects.

Chunkify Chunkify is a pretty stupid word, I guess. But it accurately describes the right way to organize the information in a PowerPoint **presentation.** You've got limited space on a **slide.** And your output medium usually doesn't allow for high information density. As a result, you need to chunkify your information. Short bulleted lists. Snappy phrases. Little nuggets of knowledge.

Clip Art Clip art refers to the pictures that you can paste onto slides as **objects.** PowerPoint figures you might just want to do this. So it provides more than 1000 clip art images. (You need to perform a complete installation to get all the images.)

In keeping with our jungle-adventure motif, here's a picture of an elephant.

continues

Clip Art *(continued)*

Adding a Clip Art Image to a Slide

To add a clip art image to a slide, follow these steps:

1 Display the slide to which you want to add the clip art image.

 2 Select the Insert Clip Art tool. Or choose the Insert Clip Art command. Either way, PowerPoint displays the Microsoft ClipArt Gallery dialog box.

3 Select a category from the drop-down list box.

4 Select one of the thumbnail sketches shown in the ClipArt Gallery dialog box. You probably won't be able to see all the images in a category without scrolling down through the list.

5 Choose OK.

Resizing Clip Art

You can use the mouse to resize clip art objects. To do this, select the object. PowerPoint marks it with selection handles. (The selection handles are those little squares.) To change the clip art object's size, drag the selection handles.

PowerPoint adds selection handles to the object or picture to show you've selected it.

Another, and usually better, way to resize clip art objects is with the Draw Scale command. Choose the Draw Scale command. When PowerPoint displays the Scale dialog box, enter a percentage in the Scale To box. A percentage greater than 100% increases the image size. A percentage less than 100% decreases the image size.

Moving Clip Art

You can easily move clip art objects with the mouse or with commands. To do this, select the clip art and then drag it to where you want it.

You can also move a clip art object using the Edit Cut and Edit Paste commands. To move clip art you've inserted, simply follow these steps:

1 Select the clip art. PowerPoint adds selection handles.

2 Choose Edit Cut.

3 If necessary, display another slide.

4 Choose Edit Paste.

Copying Clip Art

To copy clip art you've inserted, simply follow these steps:

1 Select the clip art. PowerPoint adds selection handles.

2 Choose Edit Copy.

3 If necessary, display another slide.

4 Choose Edit Paste.

Recoloring Clip Art

The colors used in a clip art object might not mesh with your color scheme. You can recolor a clip art object by selecting it, choosing the Tools Recolor command, and then using the Recolor Picture dialog box to specify the replacement colors.

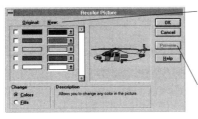

Replace an original color by activating one of these New color drop-down list boxes and making a selection.

See the effect of your re-coloring choices by choosing Preview.

Ungrouping Clip Art Components

The clip art pictures that come with PowerPoint are **vector images,** made up of individual visual elements: shapes, lines, and so on. To ungroup the elements of a clip art object—perhaps so that you can individually move or size or edit them—select the clip art and choose the Draw Ungroup command.

Clipboard Ever see the television show *Star Trek?* If you did, you might remember the transporter room. It let the *Starship Enterprise* move Captain Kirk, Mr. Spock, and just about anything else just about anywhere. The Clipboard is the Windows equivalent of the *Enterprise*'s transporter room. With the Clipboard, Windows easily moves just about anything anywhere. When working with a Windows-based **application,** you can use the Clipboard to move chunks of text, **tables,** and even graphic images to and from different **files.** You can also use the Clipboard to move text, tables, and graphic images between Windows-based applications, such as from **Microsoft Excel** to PowerPoint.

To move information around via the Clipboard, you actually use the Edit menu's Cut, Copy, Paste, and Paste Special commands. So you don't have to know all that much about the Clipboard to make good use of it. One thing you should remember about the Clipboard, however, is that it stores what you've copied or cut only temporarily. After you copy or cut, the next time you do so, the previous Clipboard contents are replaced. And when you exit Windows, the Clipboard contents are erased.

❖ **Copying Data; Moving Data; Object Linking and Embedding**

Closing PowerPoint ❖ **Exiting PowerPoint**

Closing Presentations You close **presentations** so that they don't consume memory, so that they don't clutter your screen, and so that they don't just plain annoy you.

Closing a Single Presentation

To close a single presentation, either double-click its Control-menu box or be sure the presentation is visible and then choose the File Close command.

If there are unsaved changes

PowerPoint won't close a presentation that you have changed but not yet saved. It will first ask if you want to save your changes. If you say, "Well, yeah, that seems like a good idea," PowerPoint then saves the presentation.

Color PowerPoint, as you probably know, lets you use color in your **presentations.** You might also know that PowerPoint provides professionally designed **color schemes** that look good and don't cause problems for people with color blindness.

You can change the color scheme used in a presentation, and you can change the individual colors that make up a color scheme.

One other thing. In PowerPoint, you can describe colors as combinations of **hue, saturation,** and **luminance** or as combinations of the three primary additive colors—red, green, and blue.

∴ **Troubleshooting: Your Audience Includes Men with Defective Color Vision**

Coloring Text You can change the **color** of text by using the Format Font command or by using the Text Color tool. Both methods work roughly the same. You select the **text object** you want to color. Next you choose the command or select the tool. Then you select a color from the choices PowerPoint displays.

∴ **Fonts**

Color Schemes PowerPoint **templates** and, therefore, its **presentations** use an eight-color color scheme. (The color schemes of the templates that come with PowerPoint were all created by professional designers, by the way.)

How Color Scheme Colors Are Assigned

PowerPoint uses the eight **colors** in a color scheme in the following way. Slide **backgrounds** use the first color in the scheme. Text and line objects use the second color. Shadows use the third color. Title text objects use the fourth color. Fill colors for drawn objects and shapes use the fifth color. The sixth, seventh, and eighth colors are accent colors, and they are used as the second, third, and fourth colors in **graph** objects, **organization chart** objects, and other objects you add.

Changing a Single Color in the Color Scheme

You can change one of the colors used in the color scheme. To do this, follow these steps:

1 Choose the Format Slide Color Scheme command. PowerPoint displays the Slide Color Scheme dialog box.

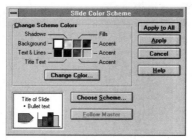

2 Click the color you want to change.

3 Choose the Change Color command button. PowerPoint displays a Color dialog box. (The dialog box title will identify the item whose color you're changing.)

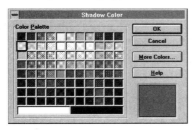

4 Click a color box.

5 Choose OK.

6 Choose the Apply command button to change the color for only the selected **slide.** Choose the Apply to All command button to change the color for all the presentation slides.

Using the More Colors command button

When a Color dialog box is displayed, you can choose the More Colors command button. PowerPoint displays the More Colors dialog box in which you specify any color—not just those displayed in the Color dialog box. With the More Colors dialog box, for example, you can specify a color by its hue, saturation, and luminance or by the parts of red, green, and blue it uses.

continues

Color Schemes *(continued)*

Changing the Color Scheme

You can select another professionally designed color scheme. To do this, follow these steps:

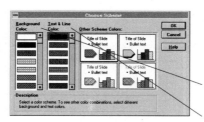

1 Choose the Format Slide Color Scheme command. PowerPoint displays the same Slide Color Scheme dialog box shown in the preceding instructions set.

2 Choose the Choose Scheme command button. PowerPoint displays the Choose Scheme dialog box.

3 Select a background color.

4 Select a text and line color.

5 Select one of the other scheme colors settings.

6 Choose OK.

7 Choose the Apply command button to change the color for only the selected slide. Choose the Apply to All command button to change the color for all the presentation slides.

Saving a Color Scheme Change

A color scheme is part of a presentation or a template. When you save the presentation or the template, you save the color scheme too.

❖ **Hue; Luminance; Saturation; Troubleshooting: Your Audience Includes Men with Defective Color Vision**

Control-Menu Commands
Control-menu commands appear, not surprisingly, on the Control menus of **application windows, document windows,** and dialog boxes.

To open the Control menu of a window or a dialog box, you click the Control-menu box. (It's the little hyphen-in-a-box in the upper left corner of the window or the dialog box.)

You use the Control-menu commands to manipulate the window or the dialog box in the following ways. (You won't always see all these commands on a Control menu. Windows displays only those that make sense in the current situation.)

Restore
Undoes the last minimize or maximize command.

Move
Tells Windows you want to move the window or the dialog box. Windows, ever mindful of your feelings, changes the mouse pointer to a four-headed arrow. After this happens, use the Up and Down direction keys to change the screen position of the window or the dialog box. Press Enter when you're finished moving.

Size
Tells Windows you want to change the size of the window. After you choose this command, Windows changes the mouse pointer to a four-headed arrow. You change the window size by using the Up and Down direction keys to move the bottom border and by using the Left and Right direction keys to move the right border. Press Enter when you're finished sizing.

Minimize
Removes the window from the screen. Windows follows your command, but to remind you of the minimized window, it displays a tiny picture, called an icon. Because you can't see the Control menu of a minimized window, simply click a minimized window icon to display its Control menu.

continues

Control-Menu Commands *(continued)*

Maximize

Tells Windows that it should make the window or the dialog box as big as it can. If you maximize an application window—such as Microsoft PowerPoint's—Windows makes the application window as big as your screen. In PowerPoint, by the way, document windows can be maximized so that they fill the application window.

Close

Removes the window or the dialog box from the screen. There's more to this command than first meets the eye, however. If you close an application window, you actually close the application. If you close a document window, you also close the presentation displayed in the document window. If a document hasn't yet been saved, most applications, including PowerPoint, will ask if you want to do this before closing the document. Closing a dialog box is the same as choosing the Cancel command button.

Next

Displays the next document window in a stack of document windows.

Switch To

Tells Windows that you want to see the Task List dialog box—presumably so that you can start another Windows-based application or so that you can move another application you've previously started to the foreground.

 Closing Presentations; Switching Tasks

Copying Data You can copy data from one **application** to another or within a Windows-based application. Copying the data places it on the **Clipboard;** you then paste the data from the Clipboard to its new location. In general, you do this by selecting the data, choosing the Edit Copy command, positioning the **insertion point** at the place you want to copy the selection, and then choosing the Edit Paste command.

Copying PowerPoint Objects

In PowerPoint, you can copy **objects** using the technique described in the preceding paragraph if you're working in Slide view. Just in case you want a blow-by-blow account, here are the precise steps:

1 Select the object you want to copy.

 2 Choose the Edit Copy command, or select the Copy tool.

3 Display the slide you want to copy the object to if you're copying to a new slide.

 4 Choose the Edit Paste command, or select the Paste tool.

Copying Text Within and Between Text Objects

In PowerPoint, you also copy text between and within text objects and outlines by copying and pasting. To do this, follow these steps:

1 Select the text you want to copy.

 2 Choose the Edit Copy command, or select the Copy tool.

3 Position the insertion point where you want the copied text inserted. Or select the text you want the copied text to replace.

 4 Choose the Edit Paste command, or select the Paste tool.

Drag-and-Drop; Moving Data; Sharing Data Between Applications

Copying Formatting You can copy the formatting used for text and the formatting used for an **object.** Both operations work in the same basic way.

Copying Text Formatting

You can copy the formatting of the selected text by using the Format Pick Up Text Style and Format Apply Text Style commands. To do so, follow these steps:

1 Select the text with the formatting you want to copy.

 2 Choose the Format Pick Up Text Style command. Or select the Format Painter tool.

3 Select the text to which you want to copy the formatting.

4 Choose the Format Apply Text Style command if you chose the Format Pick Text Style command in step 2. (You don't need to do anything in step 4 if you used the Format Painter tool.)

Copying Object Formatting

You can copy the formatting of the selected object by using the Format Pick Up Object Style and Format Apply Object Style commands. To do this, follow these steps:

1 Select the object with the formatting you want to copy.

 2 Choose the Format Pick Up Object Style command. Or select the Format Painter tool.

3 Select the object to which you want to copy the formatting.

4 Choose the Format Apply Object Style command if you chose the Format Pick Up Object Style command in step 2. (You don't need to do anything in step 4 if you used the Format Painter tool.)

Color; Fonts; Object Formatting

Cue Cards Microsoft PowerPoint includes a clever, additional type of online assistance, Cue Cards. Initially, Cue Cards is turned on when you start PowerPoint. You can close the Cue Cards window by double-clicking the Cue Cards window's Control-menu box. If you want to later restart Cue Cards, choose the Help Cue Cards command.

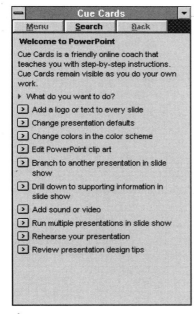

This is the Cue Cards window.

🔅 **Help**

Cursor People sometimes call the **insertion point** a cursor. You can call it that if you want. One of the fun things about being an adult is that you often get to make your own decisions. In this book, I'm going to call the insertion point an insertion point.

Whatever you do, however, don't confuse the terms insertion point and **selection cursor**.

Deleting Data You can delete an object on a slide by selecting it and then pressing the Del key or choosing the Edit Clear command.

You can delete the current text selection in a **text object**—a character, a word, or the entire contents of the text object—by pressing the Del key or the Backspace key. You can delete the preceding **character** by pressing Backspace.

You can delete the selected slide by choosing the Edit Delete Slide command.

☙ **Erasing Presentations**

Document A document is what gets displayed in the **document window** that an **application** displays. In the case of a word processor, this name works pretty nicely. The report, letter, or memo that a word processor displays in a document window inside its application window is, well, basically a document. Right?

Because this book is about PowerPoint, I should point out that what PowerPoint calls a **presentation** is, from Windows' point of view, a document.

Document Window The document window is the rectangle that an **application** uses to display your **documents.** In PowerPoint, document windows display **presentations** because PowerPoint presentations are documents.

If you have more than one document open, the **application window** stacks the documents, one on top of the other. You might not be able to see any but the active document window, however, unless you tile the open document windows or resize the top document window so that it doesn't fill the application window.

☙ **Control-Menu Commands**

Drag

Drag is a shortcut description for this three-step sequence:

1 Move the mouse pointer so that it rests over some object—such as a **text object.**

2 Press and hold down the left mouse button.

3 Move the mouse pointer. As you move, Windows moves, or drags, the object.

People in the know refer to the entire process as dragging the object. If you move a text object with the mouse, for example, you say that you dragged the text object.

Drag-and-Drop

Drag-and-Drop

Drag-and-drop is a technique that lets you move and copy pieces of a document—such as the **objects** in a presentation—with the mouse. Drag-and-drop works in many Windows-based **applications,** and it works in all **Microsoft Office** applications.

Moving with Drag-and-Drop

To move some piece of a presentation—such as a clip art picture—select it and then drag it to its new location.

Copying with Drag-and-Drop

To copy some piece of a presentation—such as a text object—select it, press and hold down Ctrl, and then drag the copy to its new location.

Moving data between applications

You can often use drag-and-drop techniques to copy data between application windows. Microsoft Word, Excel, and PowerPoint, for example, let you drag-and-drop selections between their application windows. (When you do this, you create linked objects.) This might not sound all that exciting, but drag-and-drop is a really easy way to move something you've created in one application—an Excel chart, say—to a PowerPoint presentation.

Drag; Object Linking and Embedding

Drawing
PowerPoint comes with a drawing feature. If you're the artistic type, you can add attractive drawn **objects** to the **slides** in your **presentations.** If you're not the artistic type, you can still add drawn objects to your documents. I make no promises about how they'll look, however.

Adding Drawn Objects to a Slide

To add a simple, hand-drawn graphic to a slide, you use the Drawing and Drawing+ tools. The Drawing tools appear in a vertical **toolbar** that rests along the left edge of the **application window.** If you're serious about drawing, you might as well add the Drawing+ toolbar too because it provides about a dozen other handy drawing tools you very well may want to use.

Adding toolbars

You can add any toolbar—including the Drawing+ toolbar—by choosing the View Toolbars command and then marking the check box that represents the toolbar.

Selecting Drawn Objects

 The first tool on the Drawing toolbar lets you select objects you've already drawn. You select drawn objects so that you can change them. To select an object, click the Selection tool and then the object. To select a group of objects, click the Selection tool and then draw a rectangle around the objects by dragging the mouse between the rectangle's opposite corners.

Adding Text Boxes

 Use the Text tool to add text box-drawn objects to a slide. To use the tool, select it. Then type the text you want. To place the text on two lines, press Enter where you want a line to end.

You can't add text to the outline using the Text tool. You can't, therefore, add slide titles or main headings with it.

Drawing Straight Lines

 Select the Line tool. Click where you want the line to start; then drag the mouse to where you want the line to end.

Drawing Rectangles and Squares

Select the Rectangle tool. Click where you want the upper left corner of the rectangle; then drag the mouse to where you want the lower right corner of the rectangle. Hold down the Shift key as you drag the mouse if you want to draw a square.

Drawing Ellipses and Circles

Select the Ellipse tool. Next draw an invisible rectangle that just fits the ellipses by clicking the upper left corner of the rectangle and then dragging the mouse to the lower right corner of the rectangle. PowerPoint draws an ellipse or a circle that fits in the rectangle. Hold down the Shift Key as you drag the mouse if you want to draw a circle.

Drawing Arcs

Select the Arc tool. Click where you want the arc line to start; then drag the mouse to where you want the arc line to end. If you want a 90-degree arc, hold down the Shift key as you drag the mouse.

Drawing Wild, Freeform Shapes

Select the Freeform shape tool. To draw a straight edge, click where you want the line to start, and then click where you want the line to end. To draw an edge that isn't straight, click where you want the line to start, and then trace the line by dragging the mouse. To close the shape, connect the starting and the ending points of the line edge—such as by double-clicking.

Adding AutoShapes

If you select the AutoShapes tool, PowerPoint displays the AutoShapes toolbar. It shows common shapes: arrows, balloons, stars, triangles, and so forth. To draw one of these shapes, select the AutoShapes tool that shows a picture of the shape you want to add to the slide. Then draw the shape on the slide by dragging the mouse.

To remove the AutoShapes tool, click the AutoShapes toolbar's Control-menu box.

continues

Drawing *(continued)*

Using Automatic Fill

The Fill On/Off tool is a toggle switch. When it's on, PowerPoint colors the drawn objects with the default fill color. When it's not on, drawn objects are transparent.

Telling whether the toggle's on

You can tell when the Fill On/Off toggle switch is on because it'll be depressed. No, I don't mean bummed out and looking blue. I mean it'll look pushed in. Try it. Take a peek. You'll see what I mean right away.

Using Automatic Line Coloring

The Line On/Off tool is also a toggle switch. When it's on, PowerPoint adds a colored line border to the drawn objects. When Line On/Off isn't on, drawn objects don't have a border line.

Using Automatic Shadow

The Shadow On/Off tool is *also* a toggle switch. When it's on, PowerPoint adds a shadow to the selected object.

Coloring Drawn Objects

Use the Fill Color tool on the Drawing + toolbar to change the interior colors or patterns of drawn objects.

Use the Line Color tool to change the border line color of drawn objects.

Use the Shadow Color tool to change the shadow color of drawn objects with shadows.

When you select one of the above coloring tools, PowerPoint displays a box of colored buttons. You simply click the color you want. At the bottom of the color boxes, PowerPoint also provides some other coloring options. Which colors PowerPoint displays depends on the color scheme.

D

Changing Line Style and Thickness

Use the Line Style tool to change the appearance and thickness of the lines you draw to create any object. When you select the tool, PowerPoint displays a list box of line styles. You can guess how this works, right? You simply select the line style that looks like what you want.

Using Dashed Lines

Use the Dashed Lines tool to turn a solid line into dashes or dots—or to turn a dashed line into a solid line. To use this tool, select the line and then the tool. After you select the tool, PowerPoint displays a list box of dashed line styles and a solid line. You select the line that looks like what you want.

Adding and Removing Arrowheads

To add or remove an arrowhead to or from the selected line, select the line and then the Arrowheads tool. PowerPoint displays a list box of lines with arrowheads and one line without an arrowhead. You select the list box entry with a line or an arrow that looks like what you want.

Moving Drawn Objects

You can move any object by selecting it and then dragging it.

You can restack objects that you've intentionally (or unintentionally) dog-piled on one another.

Use the Bring Forward tool to restack the dog-piled objects so that the selected object moves forward one position in the dog-pile.

Use the Send Backward tool to restack the dog-piled objects so that the selected object moves backward one layer in the dog-pile.

continues

Drawing *(continued)*

Defining dog pile

You remember what a dog pile is, right? Inexplicably, a bunch of seven-year-olds decide it'll be fun to all pile on top of one another. One kid jumps on another kid's back, and these two fall to the ground. Next other kids start jumping on the two kids who are already down. If you start drawing objects on top of one another, you don't get the grass stains, of course, but you do get a dog pile of sorts.

Grouping Drawn Objects

You can group drawn objects so that editing changes to one object in the group also get made to the other objects. To do this, select the Selection tool; then click and drag the mouse to draw a rectangle that includes all the objects you want to group.

After you select all the objects in the group, select the Group tool.

Ungrouping Drawn Objects

To ungroup previously grouped objects, select the group. Then select the Ungroup tool.

Resizing Drawn Objects

You can resize a drawn object by selecting it and then dragging its selection handles. The selection handles are those little squares that PowerPoint uses to mark the selected object.

You can also resize a drawn object by selecting it, choosing the Draw Scale command, and then entering a percentage.

Rotating Drawn Objects

You can spin, or rotate, a drawn object by selecting it and then selecting the Free Rotate, Rotate Left, or Rotate Right tool. You can manually rotate the selected object by selecting the Free Rotate tool and then dragging one of the selected object's handles.

The Rotate Left tool spins the selected drawn object 90 degrees left, or counterclockwise.

The Rotate Right tool spins the selected drawn object 90 degrees right, or clockwise.

Flipping Drawn Objects

 You can flip drawn objects horizontally or vertically. To flip a drawn object horizontally, select it and then use the Flip Horizontal tool.

 To flip a drawn object vertically, select it and then use the Flip Vertical tool.

Drill-Down Documents The term *drill-down document* is a marketing buzzword. My guess is that some young MBA at Microsoft thought it up. What it means is that if you embed and link an **OLE object** in a PowerPoint presentation, you (or somebody else) can later double-click, or *drill-down* on, the OLE object to see the entire source **document.**

If you're familiar with the mechanics of **object linking and embedding,** you already know what I'm talking about. The term *drill-down documents* describes a benefit stemming from PowerPoint's support of object linking and embedding. If you're not all that familiar with this object linking and embedding stuff, refer to its A to Z entry.

Embedding and Linking Existing Objects

Editing Text You can edit the text that makes up a PowerPoint outline by displaying Outline view and then replacing or adding to the outline text.

You can't edit the text you've typed into text boxes because that text doesn't appear on the outline. You can edit text box text by displaying Slide view, selecting the text box, and then replacing or adding to the text box text.

To replace text in Outline view, select it and then type. This works the same way as your word processor. If you know how to do this in Word or WordPerfect, you know how to do this in PowerPoint.

To add text, click where you want it and then type. Again, if you know how to do this in your word processor, you know how to do this in PowerPoint.

Drawing; Text Objects

Elevator PowerPoint, for reasons I can't fathom, refers to the scroll bar markers in its **document windows** as elevators. You know the things I mean: those little, draggable squares that appear on scroll bars.

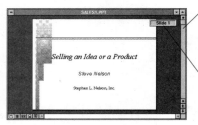

PowerPoint calls this scroll bar marker an elevator. Going up, anyone?

When you drag the elevator, PowerPoint displays a **pop-up box** that gives the slide number.

Embedding and Linking Existing Objects To create
an object using an existing file, follow these steps:

1 Choose the Insert Object command.

2 Select the Create from File option button.

3 Use the File text box to identify the object file. You need to include both the path and the file name. Or, if you don't know these, select the Browse command button to display another dialog box that provides lists of drives, directories, and files.

4 Mark the Link check box if you want Windows to update the object for subsequent file changes.

5 Mark the Display As Icon check box if you want PowerPoint to display an icon to represent the embedded object rather than a picture of the embedded object.

6 Choose OK after you finish describing the embedded or linked object. PowerPoint embeds the object into your presentation.

❖❖ Drill-Down Documents; Embedding New Objects; Graphs; Organization Charts; WordArt

Embedding New Objects To create an object from scratch using an application other than PowerPoint, follow these steps:

1 Choose the Insert Object command.

2 Be sure the Create New option button is selected.

3 Use the Object Type list box to select the Windows-based application you'll use to create the object you are about to embed.

4 Mark the Display As Icon check box if you want to see the embedded object as an icon rather than as a picture of the embedded object.

5 After you choose OK, PowerPoint starts the selected application so that you can create the object. (To see the object in your PowerPoint presentation, use the selected application's File Update command.)

⁙ **Embedding and Linking Existing Objects; Graphs; Object Linking and Embedding; Organization Charts; WordArt**

Ending Lines If you want to end a line of text and end the **paragraph** too, press Enter. If you want to end a line of text without ending the paragraph, press Shift+Enter.

Erasing Presentations **Presentations** get stored as **files** on disk. To erase a presentation file in Windows, you start the File Manager—such as by double-clicking its icon. (The File Manager icon appears in the Main program group.) Then you follow these steps:

1 Click the disk drive icon of the drive that contains the file.

2 Click the directory and if necessary double-click the subdirectory that contains the file or files you want to erase.

3 Select the presentation file or files you want to erase. PowerPoint presentation files use the file extension PPT.

4 Choose the File Delete command.

5 After File Manager asks, confirm that you do want to delete the presentation.

Unerasing Presentation Files

Exiting PowerPoint To exit just about any Windows-based **application**—including PowerPoint—you can choose the File Exit command. Or you can close the PowerPoint **application window** by double-clicking its Control-menu box. PowerPoint will ask if you want to save presentations that have unsaved changes.

Closing Presentations; Saving Presentations

Exporting Slides Exporting a slide means copying a slide so that you or a friend can use it with another **application.** You can export the selected slides as Windows metafiles, for example, which means you can use PowerPoint slides in just about any presentation or graphics application. And you can also export the text in a presentation outline, which you might do to work with the outline in a word processor.

Exporting a Windows Metafile

To create a Windows metafile based on the active slide, choose the File Save As command. After PowerPoint displays the Save As dialog box, activate the Save File As Type drop-down list box and select the Windows Metafile entry. Windows metafiles, by the way, are graphic image files. The Windows metafile format is very common. Most, and perhaps all, graphics applications can use Windows metafiles.

continues

Exporting Slides *(continued)*

Exporting an Outline as a Text File

You can export the text in the presentation outline file too. In this case, you export not only the text in the active slide but also the complete presentation outline.

To export the outline, choose the File Save As command. After PowerPoint displays the Save As dialog box, activate the Save File As Type drop-down list box and select the Outline (RTF) entry.

Exporting an Outline to Microsoft Word

You can use the Report It tool to export a PowerPoint outline to Microsoft Word with a single click of the mouse. Simply click the tool.

File

Applications and documents are stored on disk as files. For example, a presentation you create with PowerPoint gets stored on disk as a file. So does the PowerPoint application and the PowerPoint Viewer application.

File Names

You usually give a presentation its file name when you choose the File Save As command.

File-Naming Rules

MS-DOS file-naming rules apply to Windows-based application document files. A file name can't have more than eight characters. All numbers and letters that appear on your keyboard are OK. And so are many other characters. You can't, however, use characters that MS-DOS expects to be used in special ways on its command line, such as spaces, asterisks, and question marks. If you need more information than this, refer to the MS-DOS user documentation that almost surely came with your computer.

Specifying File Extensions

The MS-DOS file extension, by the way, isn't something you need to worry about. PowerPoint supplies and uses the file extension PPT to identify the document file as a presentation.

File Summary In addition to the slides you store in presentations, you can store additional information that describes the presentation itself and makes it easier to find. You collect and store this additional information by filling out the Summary Info dialog box, which PowerPoint displays any time you use the File Save As command to create a new presentation file.

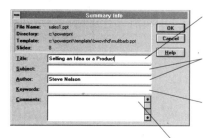

File Name:	sales1.ppt
Directory:	c:\powerpnt
Template:	c:\powerpnt\template\bwovrhd\multbarb.ppt
Slides:	8
Title:	Selling an Idea or a Product
Subject:	
Author:	Steve Nelson
Keywords:	
Comments:	

In the Title text box, enter a full, descriptive title for your presentation.

Identify the presentation subject matter and author.

Add keywords that will make it easy to later find the presentation file using the File Find File command.

Describe additional information about the presentation file using the Comments box.

Changing your mind

You can also edit the active presentation's summary information by choosing the File Summary Info command.

Finding Text Choose the Edit Find command to locate words, phrases, and other fragments of text in a presentation's **text objects** and **text boxes** and when you're working with an **outline.** To use the Edit Find command, follow these steps:

1 Select the outline area that PowerPoint should search, or don't select anything if you want PowerPoint to search the entire presentation.

2 Choose the Edit Find command. PowerPoint displays the Find dialog box.

3 In the Find What text box, specify what you're looking for.

4 Use the Match Case and Find Whole Words Only check boxes to indicate whether PowerPoint should consider case (lower vs. upper) in its search and look for whole words rather than partial words.

5 Use the Find Next command button to start and restart the search.

 **Replacing Text**

Fonts PowerPoint lets you use a variety of fonts in your **text objects** and **text boxes.** With fonts, you can even add Greek symbols and other special characters to your presentation.

Changing Fonts with Formatting Tools

The easiest way to change the fonts used in a slide is with the Formatting toolbar's tools. You can change the font, increase or decrease the point size, and add special effects such as **boldface,** underline, and *italic*. To use any of these tools, select the text you want to change and then select the Formatting toolbar tool. I describe all the Formatting toolbar tools in a table in the Quick Reference.

Changing Fonts with the Format Font Command

To change the font of the selected text with the Format Font command, follow these steps:

1 Select the text you want to change.

2 Choose the Format Font command. PowerPoint quickly displays the Font dialog box. It knows you're in a hurry.

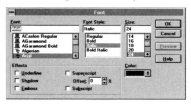

3 Select a font from the Font list box. PowerPoint identifies printer fonts with the printer icon and TrueType fonts with the Tr logo.

4 Indicate whether you want regular (roman), bold, italic, or bold italic characters using the Font Style list box.

5 Select a **point** size with the Size list box. (One point equals 1/72 inch.)

6 If appropriate, apply one or more special effects—for example, superscript or subscript—using the Effects check boxes. Shoot, even if it isn't appropriate, go ahead and experiment a bit. Live life as an adventure.

7 If you're working with a presentation in Slide view, add color using the Color drop-down list box. (The default is basic black.)

 Coloring Text

Formatting PowerPoint lets you specify the way just about any object looks on a slide.

Changing fonts and text color—**Fonts**	
Changing slide background colors and artwork—**Slide Master**	
Changing slide colors—**Color Schemes**	
Copying object borders, fill patterns, and shadows—**Copying Formatting**	
Copying text font, style, and point sizes—**Copying Formatting**	
Creating bulleted lists—**Bullets**	
Default formatting—**Slide Masters**	
Kerning—**Character Spacing**	
Specifying text alignment—**Alignment**	

Graph PowerPoint comes with the Graph application built in. Graph lets you add charts to your PowerPoint slides easily. Several **AutoLayouts,** in fact, include **placeholders** for graph **objects.**

For Microsoft Excel users

If you have Excel and know how to create charts in Excel, don't use Graph. You can create an Excel chart and then move it to a PowerPoint presentation by using drag-and-drop. Excel's charting feature is more powerful that Graph, so there's no reason for you to spend even the few minutes necessary to learn a new tool.

Adding a Chart Slide

To add a chart slide, you can follow these steps:

1 Select the Slide View button to display the Slide view of the presentation.

2 Display the slide you want the chart slide to follow.

3 Choose the Insert New Slide command. PowerPoint displays the New Slide dialog box.

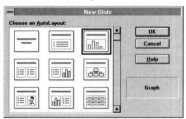

4 Select one of the slide AutoLayouts that includes a chart.

5 Choose OK. PowerPoint adds a new chart slide to the presentation.

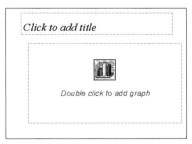

Click to add title

Double click to add graph

6 Entitle the chart slide by clicking the placeholder labeled, "Click to add title." Then type your title.

Describing the To-Be-Plotted Data

After you've added a chart slide to a presentation, you're ready to describe the to-be-plotted data. To describe your data, you enter text and numbers into the cells, or you enter the column-row intersections of the datasheet. To enter something into a cell, click it and then type. To do this, follow these steps:

1 Double-click the chart placeholder. PowerPoint opens a Datasheet window.

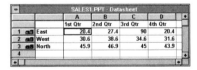

		A	B	C	D	
		1st Qtr	2nd Qtr	3rd Qtr	4th Qtr	
1	East	20.4	27.4	90	20.4	
2	West	30.6	38.6	34.6	31.6	
3	North	45.9	46.9	45	43.9	
4						

2 Replace the first column's text—East, West, and North—with textual labels describing the **graph data series.**

3 Replace the first row's text—1st Qtr, 2nd Qtr, 3rd Qtr, and 4th Qtr—with any textual labels or values identifying the **graph data categories.**

4 Fill the datasheet rows with the actual data you want to plot.

5 After you finish entering the data, double-click the Datasheet window's Control-menu box to close the window. PowerPoint displays the chart.

You can use additional graph data series and additional graph data categories by filling additional rows and columns. If you want to use fewer graph data series or fewer graph data categories, select the unneeded row or column and then choose the Edit Delete command.

continues

Graph *(continued)*

Moving the Graph Legend

The legend, which identifies the data you've plotted and names the data series, initially appears to the right of the plot area. You can move it by clicking it (to select it) and then dragging it to a new location.

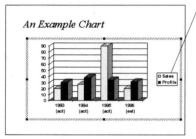

This is the legend.

Choosing a Chart Type

Although Graph chooses an initial chart type for you—a 3-dimensional column chart—you can easily choose another chart type. Click the graph object to select it—if it isn't already selected—then choose the Format Chart Type command. When you do, Graph shows pictures of all the 3-dimensional chart types. Select the 2-D Chart Dimension option button to see a list of the 2-dimensional chart types. By the way, the datasheet row number labels show pictures of the current chart type.

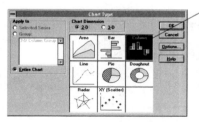

To choose a different chart type, select the picture that shows and names the chart type.

Reviewing Graph's Chart Types

Graph supplies 14 chart types, which you choose by using the Format Chart command. Which type you use depends on the visual comparison you want.

Type	What chart shows
Area	An *Area chart* plots data series as cumulative lines. The first data series' values are plotted in a line. Then the second data series' values are plotted in a line that gets stacked on top of the first line. Then the third data series' values get stacked on top of the second line, and so on.
Bar	A *Bar chart* plots each data series' values using horizontal bars. Good for comparing individual values when the chart category isn't time.
Column	A *Column chart* is like a bar chart, but it plots each data series' values as vertical bars. Good for comparing individual values when the chart category is time.
Line	A *Line chart* plots each data series' values as points on a line. Emphasizes trends in the data series' values.
Pie	A *Pie chart* plots a single data series with each value in the series represented as a pie slice. Probably the least effective chart type available because you're technically limited to a single data series and practically limited to a small number of values. (Otherwise you slice the pie into too many pieces.)
Doughnut	A *Doughnut chart* plots data series in rings, with each value in the series represented as a segment (bite) of the ring (doughnut). Coffee anyone?
Radar	A *Radar chart* plots data series using a separate value axis for each category. Value axes radiate from the center of the chart.

continues

Graph *(continued)*

Type	What chart shows
	An *XY,* or *Scatter, chart* uses two value axes to plot pairs of data points in a line. Because it visually shows the correlation between two data series, this is the most powerful and useful chart type available.
	Like its 2-dimensional cousin, the *3-D Area chart* plots data series with lines and then colors the area between the lines. Note that some of the 3-D area chart AutoFormats use the third dimension of depth to organize the data series.
	A *3-D Bar chart* plots each data series' values using horizontal solid bars. Good for comparing individual values when the chart category isn't time—but a bit imprecise.
	A *3-D Column chart* plots each data series' values as solid vertical bars. Note that some of the 3-D column chart AutoFormats use the third dimension of depth to organize the data series. Like the 3-D bar chart, a bit imprecise.
	A *3-D Line chart* should probably be called a ribbon chart. It plots each data series' values as points on a ribbon. Emphasizes trends in the data series' values, but tricky to use. (The ribbon's three-dimensionality makes it difficult to accurately gauge how fast the line rises or falls.)
	A *3-D Pie chart* plots a single data series with each value in the series represented as a pie wedge in a solid cylinder. Extremely difficult to use well. (Pie wedges in the chart background appear smaller than same-sized pie wedges in the foreground.)
	A *3-D Surface chart* plots data series as lines in a 3-dimensional grid and then colors the surface between the data series. Often useful for creating rectangular data maps. (A data map plots values on a map using latitudinal and longitudinal coordinates.)

Adding, Moving, and Removing Chart Titles

If you want, you can add text to the chart (as opposed to the slide) that describes the chart and its data. To do this, choose the Insert Titles command. After Graph displays a dialog box that in effect asks for the type of title you want to add, mark the appropriate check box. Choose OK. After PowerPoint adds a text box placeholder to the chart, type the title text you want.

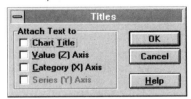

Adding and Removing Data Labels

To label the **graph data markers** with the plotted values or percentages, choose the Insert Data Labels command. After Graph displays a dialog box that in effect asks for the type of data label you want to add, select the appropriate option button and then choose OK. (In general, you only add percentage labels to pie charts.)

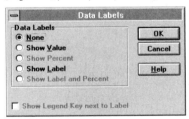

You can remove data labels by choosing the Insert Data Labels command, selecting None, and then choosing OK.

Adding and Removing Legends

If a chart doesn't already have a legend, you can add one by choosing the Insert Legend command. You can remove a legend by clicking the legend and pressing Delete.

Legend names

If you organize your to-be-plotted data into rows, Graph uses the contents of the first cell in the row to name the data in the legend.

continues

Graph *(continued)*

Adding and Removing Axes

You can use the Insert Axes command to add and remove axes. After you choose this command, Graph displays a dialog box with check boxes you use to turn on and off the display of horizontal, vertical, and—in the case of a 3-dimensional chart—depth axes.

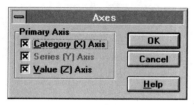

Adding and Removing Gridlines

Graph will add vertical and horizontal gridlines to the plot area. Sometimes these gridlines make it easier for chart viewers to calibrate the data markers. To add and remove gridlines from one of your charts, you can use the Insert Gridlines command. There's nothing complicated about doing this. After you choose this command, Graph displays a dialog box with check boxes you use to turn on and off the display of horizontal, vertical, and depth gridlines.

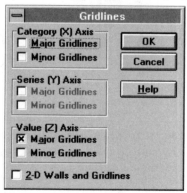

Formatting the Chart

The Format menu provides a series of commands you can use to change the way the parts of the selected chart look. In general, you do this by selecting the chart part you want to change and then choosing a command.

Returning to the PowerPoint Presentation

After you finish choosing a chart type and making any other changes to the graph, click the slide to deselect the chart object. PowerPoint changes all the menus back to the regular PowerPoint command set.

Revising an Existing Graph

If you later want to change a graph object, double-click it. Then make your changes using the mouse or the menu commands.

Graph Data Categories Data categories organize the values in a graph's data series. This sounds confusing, but let me give you an easy rule of thumb. In any graph that shows how some value changes over time, data categories are time periods. So in a chart that plots sales over a 5-year period—say, 1991 to 1995—it's the years that are the data categories.

 Graph; Graph Data Series

Graph Data Markers Data markers are the visual building blocks used to draw a chart. Different chart types use different data markers. A column chart, for example, has column data markers. A pie chart has pie-slice data markers. A line chart uses—no, wait a minute. You now know a line chart uses lines as data markers, right?

Graph

Graph Data Series A data series is simply a set of related values plotted with the same **graph data marker.** If you find the term *data series* confusing, you can use a sneaky trick to identify the data series that a chart plots. Ask yourself, "What am I plotting?" Every one-word answer will identify a data series. For example, if you ask the "What am I plotting?" question about a chart that plots sales revenue over 5 years, you can answer, "Sales." Sales then is a data series. By the way, the data markers that visually represent the sales set of values will all look similar. For example, the sales data series might be depicted with a set of red bars or as points along the same line.

⁙ **Graph; Graph Data Categories**

Guides You can choose the View Guides command to add vertical and horizontal dashed lines, or guides, to Slide view. PowerPoint marks the command with a check when you do this. You add these guides so that you can more easily and more precisely position objects.

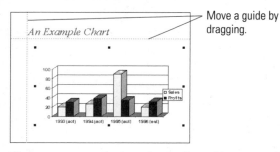

Move a guide by dragging.

If you want to make it easier to align objects to guides, choose the Draw Snap to Grid command. PowerPoint marks the command with a check. Any time you move an object edge close to a guide, Power Point moves the object so that its edge and the guide perfectly align.

Because the Draw Snap to Grid command actually makes objects snap to *guides,* I think the command name should be Snap to Guide.

⁙ **Rulers**

H

Handouts

Handouts are simply printed versions of the **slides** in a **presentation**. The slides in a handout are smaller versions of the ones you'll be using. PowerPoint lets you stick two, three, or six slides on a printed page.

You can hand out slide copies before you start a presentation. You might want to do this, for example, if you're a bit nervous and want to provide a distraction—your handout—that keeps people from focusing on your delivery, the clothing you selected, or the way you pronounce complicated words.

Printing Handouts

To print a set of handouts for the active presentation, follow these steps:

1 Choose File Print. PowerPoint displays the Print dialog box.

2 Activate the Print What drop-down list box, and select the type of handout you want.

3 Choose OK.

Help

Windows itself and Windows-based **applications** such as PowerPoint include an online help feature that means information is almost always just a click or a keystroke away. You access this help by using one of the Help menu commands. The Help menu usually appears as the rightmost menu on an application's menu bar.

Help
Contents
Search for Help on...
Index
Quick Preview
Ti**p** of the Day...
C**u**e Cards
Technical Support
About Microsoft PowerPoint...

If you have questions about one of these commands, refer to the Quick Reference.

Help Tool You can use the Help tool to get information about things you can point to. Here's how this works. First select the Help tool. PowerPoint adds a question mark to the mouse pointer arrow.

To indicate what you want help with, click on the menu command or a part of a **presentation** or a window. After you select the item you want help with, PowerPoint starts the Help **application,** and it displays any specific information about what you selected.

Hidden Slides A hidden slide is one that doesn't appear in a **slide show** unless you specifically tell PowerPoint or the PowerPoint **Viewer** that you want to see it.

Hiding a Slide

To hide a slide, you select it and then choose the Tools Hide Slide command. To show you've hidden the slide, PowerPoint places a checkmark in the front of the Tools Hide Slide command whenever the slide is selected.

You can select slides you want to hide in several ways. If you're working with Slide **view** or **Notes Pages** view, for example, you can select the slide you want to hide by displaying the slide.

If you're working with **Outline** view, you can select one or more slides by clicking and dragging.

If you're working with **Slide Sorter** view, you can select one or more slides by drawing a rectangle around the slides you want to select. To draw the selection rectangle, drag the mouse between the rectangle's opposite corners.

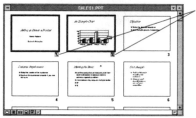

When displaying Slide Sorter view, PowerPoint flags your hidden slides by drawing a box around the slide number and then drawing a line through the box.

Displaying a Hidden Slide During a Slide Show

Even though a slide is hidden, you can still tell PowerPoint or PowerPoint Viewer that you want to see it. To indicate you want to display the next slide even though it's hidden, you can click the Hidden Slide icon, which appears in the bottom right corner of a slide whenever the next slide is hidden. (You might need to move or jiggle the mouse to get the icon to appear.) Or you can press *H* or *h*.

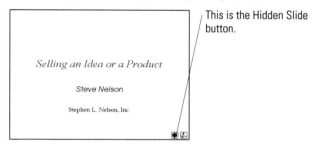

This is the Hidden Slide button.

Selling an Idea or a Product

Steve Nelson

Stephen L. Nelson, Inc.

Unhiding a Slide Permanently

To unhide a hidden slide, you select it and then choose the Tools Hide Slide command. To show you've unhidden the slide, PowerPoint removes the checkmark from the front of the Tools Hide Slide command.

Hue

What you think of as **color** is probably really hue. Green is a hue, for example. And so is red. What PowerPoint calls a color, however, is really a combination of hue, **saturation,** and **luminance.**

You don't really need to know anything about hue, saturation, and luminance, by the way, if you work with PowerPoint's predefined **color schemes.** You only need to worry about these things if you want to change individual colors in a color scheme.

Importing Documents You can open **documents** created by a word processor program and use the text to create an **outline** for a PowerPoint **presentation**. PowerPoint, for example, interprets **Microsoft Word's** outline levels, easily converting them to PowerPoint outline levels. PowerPoint can also interpret other logical outline structures—such as those that use tabs or styles to show outline levels.

You can also import slides from the presentation documents created by other presentation applications, including Harvard Graphics and Freelance.

Importing an Outline into a New Presentation

To do this, follow these steps:

1 Choose the File Open command. PowerPoint displays the Open dialog box.

2 Activate the List Files of Type drop-down list box.

3 Select the Outlines entry.

4 Describe the file's location, using the Drives and Directories list boxes, and its name, using the File Name box.

5 Choose OK.

Importing an Outline into an Existing Presentation

To do this, follow these steps:

1 Choose the Insert Slides From Outline command. PowerPoint displays the Insert Outline dialog box.

2 Describe the file's location, using the Drives and Directories list boxes, and its name, using the File Name box.

3 Choose OK.

Importing Slides from Another Application's Presentation

To do this, follow these steps:

1 Choose the Insert Slides From File command. PowerPoint displays the Insert File dialog box.

2 Activate the List Files of Type drop-down list box.

3 Select the application that created the presentation.

4 Describe the file's location, using the Drives and Directories list boxes, and its name, using the File Name box.

5 Choose OK.

In-Place Editing

If you embed an **object** created by another **application** into a PowerPoint presentation, and if that other object's application supports in-place editing, you can edit the object by double-clicking it. When you double-click the object, the menu bar of the other object's application and the application's **toolbars** replace PowerPoint's menu bar and toolbars. You can then use these menu commands and tools to edit the double-clicked object. To return the PowerPoint menu bar and toolbars, click any part of the slide except the object.

In-place editing is particularly handy with PowerPoint. You'll often use objects created with other applications in a presentation. For example, you might use a chart created in **Microsoft Excel** as the key component of an important **slide.** With in-place editing, double-clicking the embedded Excel chart would cause Excel's chart menu bar and toolbar to be displayed and made available for editing. Even though you've never started Excel. It's all pretty neat.

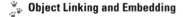 **Object Linking and Embedding**

Insertion Point The insertion point is the vertical bar that shows where what you type into a **text object** or **text box** gets placed. If this seems unclear to you, start a new **presentation,** display a **slide,** click a text object, and begin typing. See the bar that moves ahead of the text you type? That's the insertion point.

⁘ **Selection Cursor**

Italic Characters To *italicize* characters, select them and then either press Ctrl+I or select the Italic tool. You can also use the Format Font command.

⁘ **Fonts**

Kerning ⁘ **Character Spacing**

Line Spacing You can use the Format Line Spacing command to specify the amount of space between lines of text. You need to know a PowerPoint quirk to do this, however. Each **bullet** point in a PowerPoint **text object** is a **paragraph.** You create paragraphs, then, by entering some text and pressing Enter. Once you understand this paragraph business, you're ready to noodle around with line spacing. To do this, choose the Format Line Spacing command and complete the dialog box that PowerPoint displays.

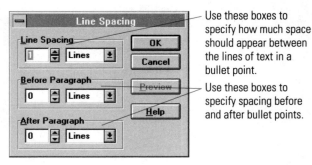

Use these boxes to specify how much space should appear between the lines of text in a bullet point.

Use these boxes to specify spacing before and after bullet points.

Linking Objects ⁛ Embedding and Linking Existing Objects

Logos You can add corporate logos to a **presentation** as long as you've got the logo stored as a graphic image—either as a **bit map image** or as a **vector image**—on disk. You add the logo to a **slide** the same way you add any **picture** to a slide. If you want the logo to appear on all the slides in a presentation, you add the picture to the **Slide Master.**

Looping Slide Shows
You can create a looping slide show—a slide show that repeats itself until you press the Esc key—by marking the Run Continuously Until 'Esc' check box, which appears in the Slide Show dialog box. The Slide Show dialog box, as you might remember, appears when you choose the View Slide Show command.

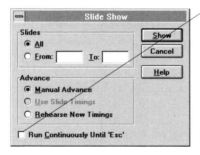

Mark this check box to create a looping slide show.

Luminance
Luminance refers to the amount of white or black in a **color.** You probably won't ever need to worry about the luminance of the colors in a **presentation,** but you can if you want to. If you want to do more than worry, you can even change a color's luminance. (You do this by using the Format Slide Color Scheme command.)

⁛ **Color; Color Schemes; Hue; Saturation**

Memory Memory is the temporary storage area your computer uses while it's running MS-DOS, Windows, and **applications.** While you're working with a PowerPoint **presentation,** for example, it's actually stored in memory. What is stored in memory is lost when you turn off your computer. So you should save stuff you want to store permanently—such as a clever presentation—by saving it on disk.

❖ **Saving Presentations**

Microsoft Excel I'm not really sure why you've looked this entry up. But I have a hunch it's because you want to use something you've created in Excel in a PowerPoint **presentation.** Perhaps a worksheet. Or maybe a chart. If you do want to do this, **drag-and-drop** the **object** you want to move.

Microsoft Mail If you've installed Microsoft Mail on your computer, you'll see a couple of new commands on the PowerPoint File menu: Send and Add Routing Slip. You can use these commands to mail a copy of the active presentation to someone else—such as your boss.

Microsoft Office This book isn't about Microsoft Office, but there's a very good chance that you acquired your copy of PowerPoint in the Microsoft Office box. Because of this, I want to mention two things. First, all the Microsoft Office **applications** work in roughly the same way. If you've worked with one application, therefore, you'll find the other applications comfortably familiar. Here's a second thing you will benefit by knowing. You can share **objects,** or chunks of **documents,** between Microsoft Office applications simply by dragging-and-dropping .

❖ **Drag-and-Drop; Sharing Data Between Applications**

Microsoft Word You can use Word and PowerPoint together in a couple of nifty ways. You can easily **drag-and-drop** an **outline** you've prepared in Microsoft Word version 6 to PowerPoint. Your Word outline becomes the PowerPoint **presentation** outline. You can also embed and link Word **documents** in PowerPoint presentations, thereby creating a **drill-down document.**

:•: **Importing Documents; Moving Data**

Movies :•: Video

Moving Data You can move data—a chunk of text or a Graph object such as a chart, for example—from one **application** to another or within a Windows-based application by cutting the data and placing it on the **Clipboard** and then pasting the data from the Clipboard to its new location.

Moving Objects and Text Within an Application

In general, you move data—both objects and text—by selecting the data, choosing the Edit Cut command (or pressing Shift+Del), positioning the **insertion point** at the place you want to move the data, and then choosing the Edit Paste command (or pressing Shift+Ins). You can also **drag-and-drop** objects and text within an **application window.** To do this, select the object you want to move; then **drag** it.

Moving Objects Between Applications

If you're moving or copying something between applications that support OLE version 2 or later, you can drag-and-drop between the application windows. To do this, select the object you want to move; then drag it to a **document window** in the other application.

continues

Moving Data *(continued)*

The easiest way to move a chart to PowerPoint

If you've created a chart in Microsoft Excel or in any other application that supports OLE version 2 or later, the easiest way to use the chart in a PowerPoint presentation is to drag-and-drop it. To do this, simply follow the steps in the preceding paragraph.

Moving Slides

You can move a slide by selecting all its objects, moving them to the Clipboard by choosing Edit Cut (or pressing Shift+Del), inserting a new blank slide by choosing Insert New Slide, and then moving the objects from the Clipboard to the new slide by choosing Edit Paste (or pressing Shift+Ins).

 Copying Data

Multitasking Multitasking refers to running more than one **application** simultaneously. You might not care about this, but Windows lets you multitask. You can be working away with your word processor, for example, at the same time that **Print Manager** is slaving away printing a PowerPoint presentation. Windows automatically multitasks Windows-based applications. Whenever you or Windows open, or start, more than one Windows-based application, you're multitasking. (Pretty cool, huh?)

To switch between the applications you're running, you use the Control menu's Switch To command. (You might want to do this if you're **moving data** between applications.)

Navigation Keys Your keyboard navigation keys can be a quick and precise way to reposition the **insertion point** when you're working with an **outline** or a **slide.** Here are a few of the navigation keys:

Key or combination	Where it moves the insertion point
Direction keys	One character or one line in the direction of the arrow
Ctrl + ←	Previous word
Ctrl + →	Next word
Ctrl + ↑	Previous slide title in Outline **view** and previous **paragraph** in Slide view
Ctrl + ↓	Next slide title in Outline view and next paragraph in Slide view
Home	Start of line
End	End of line
PgUp and PgDown	Previous page or next page
Ctrl + Home	First character in outline in Outline view or first character in current **text object** in Slide view
Ctrl + End	Last character in outline in Outline view or last character in current text object in Slide view

Notes Pages Notes Pages is another presentation **view.** Notes
Pages shows a **slide** and any notes you've attached to the
slide. Typically, you use Notes Pages as **Speaker's Notes.**
That way you'll have everything you want to say about a
particular slide on the same page as the slide.

Creating Speaker's Notes

To create Speaker's Notes using PowerPoint's Notes Pages view,
display the Notes Pages by selecting the Notes Pages View button. Or
choose the View Notes Pages command. PowerPoint displays the
Notes Pages View window.

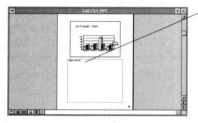

Enter the Speaker's
Notes you want for the
slide here. You probably
will not be able to read
the tiny type unless you
use the Zoom tool to
magnify the window.

Printing Speaker's Notes

To print Speaker's Notes, choose the File Print command, activate the
Print What drop-down list box and select the Notes Pages entry, and
then choose OK.

Printing Presentations; Rehearsing

Object The information that appears on a PowerPoint slide consists of objects. In essence, these objects are simply the
building blocks that make up the slide. Chunks of **text.** A
piece of **clip art. Tables.** Perhaps even a chart or two.

To make this book as understandable as possible (and to
keep both of us from getting confused), I'll always identify the type of object I'm talking about, okay? If I'm talking about a chunk of text on a slide—say, a short bulleted
list—I'll refer to it as a **text object.** If I'm talking about a
piece of clip art, I'll refer to it as a clip art object. And if
I'm talking about an object you've created with another
application and then embedded into a PowerPoint presentation using **Object Linking and Embedding** (OLE),
I'll refer to it as an **OLE object.**

O

Object Formatting Much of the formatting available within a
presentation applies to the **objects** that constitute a slide.
In those big books on PowerPoint, the authors spend
many, many pages describing all the fancy-schmancy object formatting you can do. Here, however, I'll simply
quickly review the major types of object formatting.

Adding an Object Border

To draw a border line around the selected object, choose the Format
Colors and Lines command.

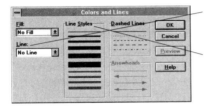

Activate the Line drop-
down list box, and select
a line color.

Select a line thickness
from the Line Styles list.

Select a dashed border
line, if you want.

Changing Object Fill, or Background, Patterns

To color the background of the selected object, choose the Format
Colors and Lines command. Activate the Fill drop-down list box, and
select a background color from the choices displayed. To color an
object's background the same as the slide background, select the
Background option from the Fill list box.

Adding Object Shadows

To add a shadow or embossing to the selected object, choose the
Format Shadow command. Activate the Color drop-down list box, and
select the shadow color. To also specify the size and placement of the
shadowing, use the Offset option buttons. For a 6-point shadow along
the right and bottom edges of the object, for example, mark the Down
and Right option buttons and enter 6 into the Points boxes. (Embossing
uses light shadowing and background patterns to give objects a raised,
3-dimensional look.)

continues

Object Formatting *(continued)*

Resizing an Object

You can easily change the size of the selected object by choosing the Draw Scale command. After you choose this command, PowerPoint displays a dialog box that lets you make several scaling, or size, changes.

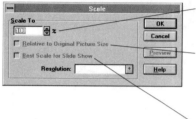

Specify the new size of the selected object as a percentage.

Indicate if the scaling should be relative to the object's original size rather than to its current size.

This check box tells PowerPoint to optimally scale **movies** during a slide show.

You usually don't need to worry about the Resolution setting. PowerPoint takes care of this for you automatically.

Object Linking and Embedding Object linking and embedding, or OLE, is a Microsoft enhancement to Windows.

What OLE Does

You use OLE to create what's called a compound document—a document file that combines two or more types of documents. For example, you might want to create a compound document that includes a long report written in, for example, Microsoft Word. On page 27 of your report, however, you might want to include a worksheet (or a worksheet fragment) created in Lotus 1-2-3. And perhaps on page 37 of your report, you might want to include a chart created in Microsoft Excel. So your compound document really consists of stuff—called **objects**—created in different applications and pasted together into one big, compound document.

Using OLE to Create Compound Documents

To do all this pasting together and combining, you can often use the application's Edit Copy and Edit Paste (or Edit Paste Special) commands. **Microsoft Office** applications such as PowerPoint include an Insert Object command that lets you add and create objects for a compound document. You indicate whether you want an object linked or embedded when you use the Edit Paste, Edit Paste Special, or Insert Object command. (Microsoft Office applications also let you drag-and-drop objects between applications.)

Distinguishing Between Linked Objects and Embedded Objects

A linked object—remember this might be the Excel worksheet you've pasted into a PowerPoint presentation—gets updated whenever the source document changes. An embedded object doesn't. (You can, however, double-click an embedded object to open the application that created the embedded object and make your changes.)

What you absolutely need to know about OLE

Perhaps the most important tidbit for you to know about OLE is that it's very easy to use. You don't have to do anything other than copy and paste the objects you want to plop into the compound document. If you're working with applications that support version 2 or later of OLE, you can drag-and-drop objects between application windows.

> Application Windows; Drag-and-Drop; In-Place Editing; Moving Data

OLE Objects OLE is an acronym for **Object Linking and Embedding.** An OLE object, then, is an **object** you've plopped into a PowerPoint presentation using Object Linking and Embedding. **Graph** and **Microsoft Excel** charts, **Microsoft Word** tables, and **organization charts,** for example, are all OLE objects.

Opening Presentations

Opening Presentations You open PowerPoint presentations so that you can modify or view the presentations. To do this, you usually use PowerPoint's File Open command. Here's how the process works:

1 Choose the File Open command.

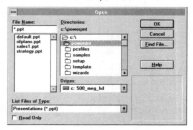

2 Enter the presentation's file name.

3 If necessary, use the Directories and Drives list boxes to specify where the file is located.

4 Choose OK.

Organization Charts PowerPoint comes with a separate application, Microsoft Organization Chart for Windows, that lets you embed organization charts, as **OLE objects,** in PowerPoint slides.

Adding an Organization Chart Slide

To add an organization chart slide, follow these steps:

1 Select the Slide View button to display the Slide view of the presentation.

2 Display the slide you want the organization chart slide to follow.

3 Choose the Insert New Slide command. PowerPoint displays the New Slide dialog box.

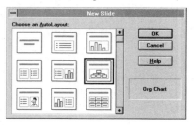

4 Select the slide autolayout that includes an organization chart.

5 Choose OK. PowerPoint adds a new organization chart slide to the presentation.

6 Entitle the organization chart by double-clicking the text box la-beled, "Click to add title." Then type your title.

Building the Organization Chart

To build the organization chart, double-click the organization chart icon. (This icon is actually an embedded organization chart OLE object.) PowerPoint starts the Organization Chart for Windows application.

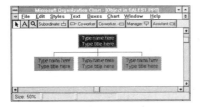

Fill in the organization chart boxes by selecting them and then typing names and positions. You stick the name on the first line of the box and the position on the second line of the box. Organization chart boxes also provide space for comments, but these don't show unless the box is selected.

To add boxes to the organization chart, use the Subordinate, Co-worker, Manager, and Assistant buttons, which appear beneath the menu bar. To use any of these buttons, first select the existing position to which you'll connect the new box. Then select the button.

After you finish building the organization chart, choose the File Exit and Return To command to return to the PowerPoint application.

Outline An outline is simply another **view** of a **presentation.** It shows the text from **text objects** in your presentation—slide titles, bulleted list points, and so forth. But it doesn't show visual elements such as drawn objects, nor does it show OLE objects, such as organization charts. (An outline also doesn't show the text you've entered in **text boxes** using the Drawing toolbar's Text tool.)

You can create an outline from scratch. Or you can modify the outline proposed by the AutoContent Wizard. Either way, as part of outlining your presentation, you do two things. You provide titles for each slide in your presentation. And you enter any additional text you want slides to show—for example, bulleted lists. People who don't feel constrained by the rules of standard grammar call this process "chunkification." These same people like to say they "**chunkify.**"

Switching to Outline View

To switch to Outline view, click the Outline View tool. Or choose the View Outline command.

Creating an Outline in Microsoft Word

If you've created an outline in Microsoft Word version 6 and want to use it as the basis of a PowerPoint presentation, you can do so. There are several ways to do this, but the easiest method available is to **drag-and-drop** the outline from the Word application window to the PowerPoint application window. All you need to do is view the Microsoft Word document in Outline view before selecting it for the drag-and-drop.

Another way to move a Word outline to PowerPoint is by importing the Word document. You do this by opening the Word document from inside PowerPoint.

When you import Microsoft Word outlines

Microsoft Word allows up to nine levels in an outline. But PowerPoint allows only five levels. If you import a Word document with more than five levels, PowerPoint treats the sixth-, seventh-, eighth-, and ninth-level entries as fifth-level entries.

Creating an Outline in Another Word Processor

If you've created an outline in another word processor, you can use it as the basis of a PowerPoint presentation too. All you need to do is save the word processing document in an RTF file in which you've used heading styles. (RTF stands for "rich text format" and is a common file format for word processing files.) Or you can save the word processing document in an ASCII text file in which you've used tab indentions to indicate outline levels.

After you've got this RTF or ASCII text file ready, you import it. To do this, you simply open the document from inside PowerPoint.

Creating an Outline from Scratch

If you use the AutoContent Wizard to start a presentation, PowerPoint displays a boilerplate outline using Outline view. Enter the slide titles as the highest level in your outline. A bulleted list that goes on a slide would be entered as the next lower level for that slide. End each line of text—slide titles, bullet points, whatever—by pressing Enter.

A slide title.

A heading, which happens to be a bullet point.

This is the way the second slide looks.

You can replace or edit slide titles, headings, and subheadings. Select a slide title by clicking the slide icon, and select a bullet point by clicking the bullet.

Select text by clicking and dragging the mouse. Replace selected text by typing over it. This text selection and entry business works the same basic way as it does with a word processor. If you know how to select text in Word, you know how to select text in PowerPoint.

continues

Outline *(continued)*

Working with Title Slides

A title slide has only a title and, optionally, a subtitle. It doesn't have, for example, a bulleted list. If you enter a second level of text beneath the title slide's title, PowerPoint assumes what you've entered is the subtitle.

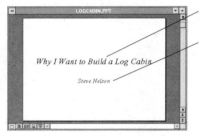

This is the title slide's title.

This is the title slide's subtitle.

Using the Outline Tools

The outlining toolbar provides a series of buttons useful for creating and revising outlines. Remember that the highest level in an outline is the slide.

⬅	Promotes selected line to next higher outline level
➡	Demotes selected line to next lower outline level
⬆	Moves selected line so that it's in front of the preceding line
⬇	Moves selected line so that it's behind the following line
➖	Hides, or collapses, next lower outline level
➕	Displays next lower outline level if it's previously been hidden, or collapsed
⬆☰	Displays all slide titles in outline
⬇☰	Displays all stuff in outline
ᴬ𝐴	Turns on and off any text formatting

Moving Slides with the Mouse

You can move a slide by clicking its icon and then dragging it up or down. When you begin to drag the slide icon, PowerPoint changes the pointer to a double-headed arrow.

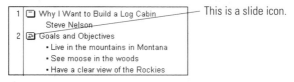

This is a slide icon.

Importing Documents; Navigation Keys; Printing Presentations

Overtyping Normally, Windows-based **applications** let you insert the characters you type at the **insertion point** or let you replace, or overtype, characters that follow the insertion point. And, normally, to toggle between character insertion and character overtyping, you press the Ins key. In PowerPoint, however, character overtyping doesn't exist. Any text you type will always be inserted. When you want to replace text, therefore, select the text you want to type over and then type.

Paragraphs In prose, a paragraph is a group of sentences. Ideally, it starts with a topic sentence and develops a single thought. High school composition, so I hear, was a breeze if you could write solid, well-structured paragraphs.

In PowerPoint, a paragraph is simply a chunk of text in a **text object** that ends where you press Enter. Almost always, then, each of your bullet points are paragraphs.

This might all seem like much ado about nothing, but you should remember what paragraphs are—at least from PowerPoint's point of view. The reason is that much of the **formatting** you do in PowerPoint applies to paragraphs. You can, for example, format paragraphs, or bullet points, by changing indention, **line spacing,** and **alignment.**

Ending Lines

Paragraph Spacing ❖ Line Spacing

Periods You can add periods to and remove periods from the ends of the selected **paragraphs.** Choose the Format Periods command so that PowerPoint displays the Periods dialog box. Then select either the Add Periods or Remove Periods option button and choose OK.

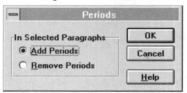

Pick A Look Wizard The Pick A Look Wizard helps you select a template that's appropriate to your presentation message and the output medium. To do this, the Pick A Look Wizard steps you through nine dialog boxes.

Starting the Pick A Look Wizard

You can start the Pick A Look Wizard and use it to modify the design of the open presentation by choosing the Format Pick A Look Wizard command or by selecting the Pick A Look Wizard tool.

You can start the Pick A Look Wizard and use it to specify the design of a brand-new presentation by starting PowerPoint and selecting the Pick A Look Wizard option button in the PowerPoint dialog box. Or, if PowerPoint is already running, you can start the wizard by choosing the File New command or by selecting the New tool and selecting the Pick A Look Wizard option button in the New Presentation dialog box.

After you've started the Pick A Look Wizard, you'll see the first Pick A Look Wizard dialog box.

Running the Pick A Look Wizard

1 Select Next in the first Pick A Look Wizard dialog box to get things rolling and to display the second dialog box.

2 Indicate the output medium you'll use. This is important because the output medium you'll use largely determines which type of color scheme the presentation should use.

3 Select Next. The wizard displays the third dialog box.

4 Select a template design for the presentation by selecting one of the option buttons in the third dialog box. Which options you see depends on the output medium choice you made in step 2. The preview box in the left half of the dialog box shows what the selected option looks like.

continues

Pick A Look Wizard *(continued)*

5 Select Next. The wizard displays the fourth dialog box.

6 Use the check boxes provided by the fourth Pick A Look Wizard dia-
log box to indicate what your presentation should include:
Full-Page Slides, Speaker's Notes, Audience Handout Pages, and
Outline Pages.

7 Select Next. The wizard displays the fifth dialog box.

8 Use the check boxes provided by the fifth Pick A Look Wizard dialog box to indicate whether you want your name (or your company
name or other text), the date, and the page number displayed at
the bottom of every slide. If you mark the Name check box, of
course, be sure to enter your name in the box provided.

9 Select Next. The wizard displays the sixth dialog box, which looks
almost identical to the fifth dialog box.

10 Use the check boxes provided by the sixth Pick A Look Wizard dialog box to indicate whether you want your name (or your company
name or other text), the date, and the page number displayed at
the bottom of every page of your Speaker's Notes. If you're feeling
a funny sense of déjà vu, it's because this step mirrors step 8.

11 Select Next. The wizard displays the seventh dialog box, which looks almost identical to the fifth and sixth dialog boxes.

12 Use the check boxes provided by the seventh Pick A Look Wizard dialog box to indicate whether you want your name (or your company name or other text), the date, and the page number displayed at the bottom of your audience handout pages.

13 Select Next. The wizard displays the eighth dialog box, which looks darn similar to the last three dialog boxes you've seen.

14 Use the check boxes provided by the eighth Pick A Look Wizard dialog box to indicate whether you want your name (or your company name), the date, and the page number displayed at the bottom of every page of your outline. And now I'm beginning to feel a funny sense of déjà vu.

15 Select Next. The wizard displays the ninth dialog box. Ah. The checkered flag.

16 Select Finish. The wizard ends. Your presentation now uses the new look. (To see the new look, switch to Slide **view**.)

Pictures You can add pictures to **slides** as long as the picture file is stored in a recognizable format. (Which files are *recognizable* depends on which graphics filters you installed when you set up PowerPoint.) This means you aren't limited to using **clip art.** You can also use output from drawing programs and even scanned photographs.

continues

Pictures *(continued)*

Inserting Pictures

To add a picture to a slide, follow these steps:

1 Select the picture **placeholder** if it exists. (If a picture placeholder doesn't exist, PowerPoint places your picture in the middle of the slide.)

2 Choose the Insert Picture command.

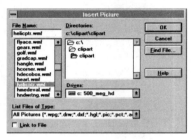

3 In the Insert Picture dialog box, use the File Name list box to identify the picture file.

4 Use the Directories and Drives list boxes to find the picture file.

5 Use the List Files of Type drop-down list box to specify which types of picture, or graphic, files you want to see listed. (Picture file types are distinguished by file extensions, so selecting a type actually tells PowerPoint to list only those files with the specified extension.)

6 To link the picture to the document file, mark the Link to File check box. (This adds the picture to your document as a linked object. Windows updates the document picture whenever the picture file changes.) If you link the picture, you don't have to save the picture in the document. (This makes the document file smaller—which is good—but also means that you won't be able to see the picture until you update the link using the Edit Links command.)

Resizing Pictures

You can use the Draw Scale command to resize the picture **object.**
(This works as described in the **Object Formatting** entry.)

You can also use the mouse to resize pictures. To do this, select the
picture object. PowerPoint marks the picture with selection handles.
(The selection handles, as you might already know, are those little
squares.)

To change the picture's
size, drag the selection
handles.

Moving Pictures

To move a picture, select it by clicking. Then drag the picture to a new
location.

Removing Pictures

To remove a picture from a slide, select the picture object. Then press
Del.

Copying Pictures

To duplicate a picture on a slide, select the picture object, choose the
Edit Copy command or the Copy tool, choose the Edit Paste command
or the Paste tool, and then move the new picture. (After you copy and
paste a picture as described here, PowerPoint places the new picture
on top of the old picture.)

Placeholders As part of adding a new **slide** to a **presentation,** you choose an **AutoLayout.** This AutoLayout includes slots, or holes, into which you can plop the information that you want on the slide. A bulleted list. A graph. A table. You get the idea. Of course, this information doesn't exist until you add it, so until you do add it, PowerPoint displays a placeholder. This placeholder includes a rectangle with a dashed line border, oftentimes a picture of whatever you'll ultimately add, and the instructions to click or double-click the placeholder when you want to add the information.

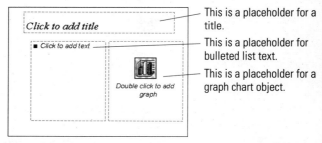

This is a placeholder for a title.

This is a placeholder for bulleted list text.

This is a placeholder for a graph chart object.

After you actually stick an **object** into the slot, you'll see the object in place of the placeholder.

Play Lists A play list is a list of slide shows you want PowerPoint to play, or show. I'm not going to go into all the specifics of how you create and use play lists here. But let me give you the bird's-eye view. To create a play list, you create a text file that lists the full path and file names of the presentations you want shown. (Save the text file with an extension of LST.) Then to run a gigantic slide show that uses each of the listed presentations, you open the text file rather than a presentation. For more information about play lists, refer to the play list topic in PowerPoint's online help file.

Pointer The pointer is the arrow that moves across your screen as you roll the mouse across your desk.

Oh-oh. What's that? You don't have a mouse? OK. If you have some other kind of pointing device, such as a trackball, the pointer is the arrow that moves across your screen as you noodle around with this other, unidentified pointing device.

I should also mention that Windows-based **applications** such as PowerPoint will change the look of the pointer as a secret signal to you about what they're doing. If PowerPoint is busily working at some time-consuming task, the pointer might look like a tiny hourglass.

Points One point equals 1/72 inch. In Windows-based **applications** such as PowerPoint, you often specify sizes in points. **Fonts** get sized this way, for example.

Pop-up Box A pop-up box looks like a message box, but it doesn't have a title bar, and it doesn't have a Control menu. For example, when you drag the **elevator** in Slide view, PowerPoint displays a pop-up box that shows the number of the **slide** to which you've moved.

Presentation The **document** you create in PowerPoint is called a presentation. It includes **slides, handouts, Speaker's Notes,** and your **outline.** A presentation gets stored on disk in a single **file.**

Presentation Templates ⁘ **Template**

Present It You can add the Present It button to one of the **Microsoft Word** toolbars. The Present It tool lets you easily export a Word **outline** to a PowerPoint **presentation.** Unfortunately, adding the Present It button is rather cumbersome. So you won't want to do this unless you're pretty familiar with how toolbar customization works. Refer to the Microsoft Word version 6 user documentation for more information.

 Importing Documents

Printing Presentations You can print presentations, of course. All you need to do is choose the File Print command or select the Print tool. If you select the Print tool, PowerPoint immediately prints copies of the slides in your presentation.

If you choose the File Print command, PowerPoint displays the Print dialog box. It allows you to choose what you want to print from among several presentation **views: slides,** several **handout** formats, **Notes Pages,** or your **outline.**

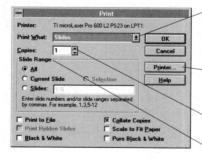

Use the Print What drop-down list box to specify which presentation view you want printed.

Use the Printer command button to change the printer setup.

You've guessed what the Copies box does, right?

The Slide Range options let you print a subset of the presentation's slides.

What really happens when you print

When you tell an application (such as PowerPoint) to print some
document (such as a presentation), what really happens is that the
application creates a printable copy of the document (called a spool
file in case you care) and then sends this printable copy to another
application, Print Manager. Print Manager then prints the document.

Rehearsing

To help you rehearse a **presentation**, PowerPoint
will turn on a timer that counts the seconds you display
each **slide**. If you save the slide timings, you can use the
results of rehearsal timing to run a presentation.

Timing a Rehearsal

To turn on this rehearsal timer, use the View Slide Show command to
start a **slide show** and select the Rehearse New Timings option
button. Then select Show and rehearse your presentation.

As you rehearse, PowerPoint tracks the time. Tick-tock, tick-tock.
(You'll see a button in the lower left corner of your screen that shows
the minutes and seconds a slide has been displayed.) After you finish
the presentation, PowerPoint displays a message box that tells you
how long your presentation took and asks if you want to record the
new slide timings in **Slide Sorter** view.

If you indicate you do want to record the slide timings in Slide Sorter
view, PowerPoint displays them beneath the slides.

Using Slide Timings to Run a Presentation

You can use recorded slide timings to run a presentation. To do this,
use the View Slide Show command to start a slide show and select
the Use Slide Timings option button. Then select Show.

Replacing Fonts You can change a **font** used in a **presentation** in one fell swoop. Simply choose the Tools Replace Fonts command. PowerPoint displays the Replace Font dialog box.

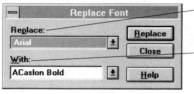

Specify the font you want to replace using this drop-down list box.

Specify the new font you want using this drop-down list box.

Select Replace to make your change.

∴ Slide Master

Replacing Text In both Slide and Outline views, you can choose the Edit Replace command to locate and replace text in **text objects** and **text boxes.** To use the Edit Replace command, follow these steps:

1 Choose the Edit Replace command.

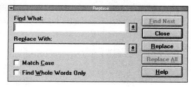

2 Use the Find What text box to specify what you want to replace.

3 Use the Replace With text box to specify the replacement text.

4 Use the Match Case and Find Whole Words Only check boxes to indicate whether PowerPoint should consider case (lower vs. upper) in its search and look for whole words rather than partial words.

5 Select Find Next to start and restart the search.

6 Select Replace to substitute the replacement text.

7 Select Replace All to substitute the replacement text without your intervention.

Limiting replacement

In Outline view, you can limit the replacement by selecting a block of outline text before you choose the Edit Replace command. If you don't select a block of text, PowerPoint searches through the entire presentation and gives you the option of replacing text throughout the document.

∴ Finding Text

Report It You can select the Report It tool to export the active **presentation's** outline to **Microsoft Word.** After you select the tool, PowerPoint starts Microsoft Word and creates a new Word **document** with the PowerPoint **outline.**

Rulers You can choose the View Ruler command to add vertical and horizontal rulers to Slide view. You add rulers so that you can more easily and more precisely position **objects.**

∴ Guides

Saturation Saturation refers to the pureness of a color—how much it differs from gray. You probably won't need to work with color saturation settings. But PowerPoint gives you the ability to do this when necessary by changing the characteristics of individual **colors** used in a **color scheme.** You use the Format Slide Color Scheme command to do this.

⁖ **Hue; Luminance**

Saving Presentations You can save the **presentations,** or documents, that PowerPoint creates. To do this, you use the File Save As and File Save commands.

Saving a Presentation for the First Time

To save a presentation for the first time, you follow these general steps:

1 Choose the File Save As command or the Save tool. PowerPoint displays the Save As dialog box.

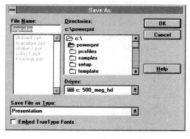

2 Enter a **file name.** You need not supply a file extension. PowerPoint supplies the extension PPT as a way of identifying the file as a PowerPoint presentation.

3 Use the Directories and Drives list boxes to specify where the file should be located.

S

4 If you will view the presentation on another computer with the
Viewer application and you're not sure whether this other computer has all the **TrueType** fonts you've used, mark the Embed
TrueType Fonts check box. This will make your presentation file
larger, but it'll also mean the presentation will use all the right
fonts.

5 Choose OK.
6 Enter a **file summary**.
7 Choose OK.

Saving a Presentation with a New Name or in a New Location

To save a presentation with a new name or in a new location, use the
File Save As command as described in the preceding step sequence.
Remember to specify the new name or location.

Resaving a Presentation

To save a modified version of a presentation file you've already saved
once before, you choose the File Save command or use the Save tool.
After you do this, the application replaces the original, saved-to-disk
file with what's in memory and displayed on your screen.

Selecting Data To change some fragment of text, an **object**
you've drawn, or an embedded **OLE object** you've used in
a **slide,** you'll first need to select it. The easiest way to do
this is by clicking it with the mouse. (In fact, if you don't
have a mouse, your next best investment in computer
hardware is a mouse.)

If the thingamajig you want to change is an OLE object,
you should double-click it to select the object and at the
same time tell PowerPoint you want the creating
application's menu commands available for **in-place editing.**

Selection Cursor The selection cursor marks the selected option in a dialog box or the selected text in a box. How Windows marks items with the selection cursor depends on the item being marked.

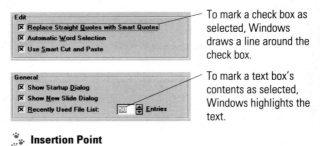

To mark a check box as selected, Windows draws a line around the check box.

To mark a text box's contents as selected, Windows highlights the text.

∴ **Insertion Point**

Shadows ∴ **Object Formatting**

Sharing Data Between Applications You can easily share data between Windows-based **applications.** You can move worksheets and charts you've created in **Microsoft Excel** or Lotus 1-2-3 to PowerPoint, for example. And you can move tables or textual blurbs you've created in a word processor such as **Microsoft Word** or WordPerfect to PowerPoint too.

Using Edit Copy and Edit Paste

To share data between applications, you follow these general steps:

1 Select what you want to share: a worksheet range, a chart, a chunk of text, a value, or anything else.

2 Choose the application's Edit Copy command.

3 Switch to the other application using the Control menu's Switch To command.

4 Place the **insertion point** where you want to place the copied data.

5 Paste the contents of the **Clipboard** at the insertion point location. (Probably, you'll do so with that application's Edit Paste or Edit Paste Special command.)

To link or to embed—that is the question

When you choose Edit Paste Special to paste an object—a worksheet fragment, for example—into another application's document, you'll usually have a choice as to whether the pasted object is linked to the source document or is merely an embedded copy of the source document.

Using the Mouse to Drag-and-Drop

If two applications support Object Linking and Embedding version 2 or later, you can also share data by dragging-and-dropping. To do this, start both applications and open the documents that will share data. Then select the chunk of information you want to share in the source document and drag it to the compound document.

Drag-and-Drop; Object Linking and Embedding; Switching Tasks

Shortcut Menus A mostly cool new feature you're seeing in many Windows-based **applications,** including PowerPoint, is the shortcut menu. Here's the scoop in case you don't already know. Many applications are now smart enough to know which commands make sense in which situations. Many applications also know which commands you, as a user, are most likely to use in those situations. If you want them to, many applications will display a menu of these commands—called the shortcut menu. All you need to do is click the right button on the mouse. (Remember that you use the left mouse button for selecting menus, commands, dialog box elements, and assorted and sundry items.)

Slide Buttons You can use the PgDown and PgUp keys to move through the **slides** in a **presentation** when you're in Slide view. Or you can use the Slide buttons. Or you can use the **elevator.**

This is the Previous Slide button.

This is the Next Slide button.

Slide Master The Slide Master, in effect, stores several pieces of design information about the way your slides should look. It stores and allows you to change **background** color. (You can also change the background color by adjusting the **color scheme.**) The Slide Master stores and allows you to change **objects** such as picture objects or clip art objects that you want to appear on every slide. And it stores and allows you to change the default text formatting used for each **outline** level of text.

Viewing a Slide Master

To look at the Slide Master for a presentation, choose the View Master command and select Slide Master. Or hold down Shift and select the Slide View tool.

This is a master slide. Each presentation has its own Slide Master.

Adjusting the Background Color

To adjust the background color of a Slide Master, choose the Format Slide Background command to display the Slide Background dialog box.

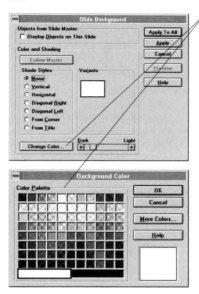

Select the Change Color command button to display a dialog box of color buttons. Then select the color button from the Color Palette.

About the color scheme background color

When you change the background color of a Slide Master, you change the background color in the color scheme.

Changing Text Formatting

You can change the formatting of any outline level of text. To do this, select the outline level you want to change. Then choose the appropriate Format menu command. To change the **font,** for example, choose the Format Font command. You can also change other elements of text formatting such as **alignment, bullets, case, line spacing,** and **periods.**

continues

Slide Master *(continued)*

Adding Objects to a Slide Master

You can add **drawing** objects, **clip art** objects, and **picture** objects to a Slide Master. What you add to a Slide Master appears on each slide in the presentation. You add objects to a Slide Master the same way you add objects to any other slide.

Editing Existing Slide Master Objects

If you're working with a Slide Master that comes from one of the templates that come with PowerPoint, it might already have objects. You can edit these objects after ungrouping them. To ungroup them, you use the Drawing toolbar's Ungroup tool.

Adding Times, Dates, and Slide Numbers to a Slide Master

Use the Insert Time command to add the time to a Slide Master. The time appears as a double colon (::) inside a frame. Drag the frame to reposition it.

Use the Insert Date command to add the date to a Slide Master. The date appears as a double slash (//) inside a frame. Drag the frame to reposition it.

Use the Insert Page Number command to add the slide number to a Slide Master. The slide number appears as a double pound sign (##) inside a frame. Drag the frame to reposition it.

Times, dates, and page numbers appear on slides during slide shows and get printed. They don't appear in Outline or Slide **views,** however.

Slide Numbers
You can add numbers to **slides** by inserting page numbers on a **Slide Master.** You can determine where slide numbering starts by adjusting the **slide setup.**

Slides   A slide is a page in a **presentation.** It can show just about anything: text, **graphs, organization charts, tables, objects** you've drawn, **clip art,** and even **OLE objects** you've created in other **applications.** You can show the slides in a presentation on your computer screen. You can print the slides in a presentation in black and white on a regular printer or as color transparencies if you've got a color-capable printer. Or, if you want to get really fancy, you can create **35mm slides** using either a film recorder or a service bureau.

⁂ **Text Box; Text Object**

Slide Setup   When you want to print a presentation's slides or create **35mm slides** for presentation, you should first use the File Slide Setup command to specify the appropriate slide size, where slide numbering should start, and the slide orientation.

After you choose the File Slide Setup command, PowerPoint displays the Slide Setup dialog box.

Select an appropriate slide size.

If you want a custom slide size, use these boxes to specify the custom size.

⁂ **Printing Presentations; Slide Numbers**

Slide Show

When you want to display the slides in a presentation, you run a slide show. You can run a slide show with PowerPoint itself. Or you can run a slide show with **Viewer.**

Running a Slide Show with PowerPoint

You can run a slide show in the usual way by opening the presentation and then selecting the Slide Show View button.

You can also run a slide show with PowerPoint by opening the presentation and then choosing the View Slide Show command. After PowerPoint displays the Slide Show dialog box, use it to indicate how you want the slide show run.

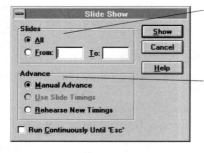

Use the Slides option buttons to indicate whether you want all the slides shown or only a subset of the slides.

Use the Advance option buttons to indicate what should trigger the display of a new slide.

Choose Show when you're ready to go.

Running a Slide Show with Viewer

To run a slide show with the PowerPoint Viewer, start Viewer. When Viewer displays the Microsoft PowerPoint Viewer dialog box, identify the presentation using the File Name, Directories, and Drives boxes. To start the slide show, choose Show.

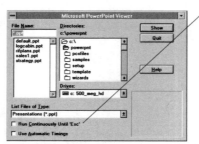

If you want the slide show to run until someone presses Esc, mark this check box.

Slide Sorter

The Slide Sorter, which is one of the presentation views available, is like a light table on which you organize and order the **slides** in a **presentation.** To view a presentation using Slide Sorter view, choose the View Slide Sorter command. Or select the Slide Sorter view button.

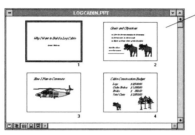

This is Slide Sorter view.

To rearrange slides, drag them.

To delete a slide, select it and choose Edit Delete Slide.

Moving and copying slides between presentations

You can move and copy slides between presentations. Display the two presentations in side-by-side document windows showing Slide Sorter view. To move a slide, drag the slide between the presentation document windows. To copy a slide, hold down the Ctrl key and drag the slide between the presentation document windows.

Drag-and-Drop

Slide Titles

If you're using Outline view, you enter slide titles as the first outline level. If you're using Slide view, you enter slide titles in the **placeholder** labeled, "Click to add title."

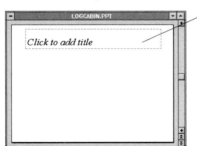

Click to add title

To add a title to a slide, click here and type the title. To replace an existing title, select the title text and then type.

Outline; Slides; Text Object; Views

Slide-to-slide Transitions ⁛ **Transition**

Sound You can add sound to a presentation by inserting a Sound Recorder **OLE object** or some other application's sound-producing object.

Speaker's Notes Speaker's Notes are like word processing documents you create for your speech. The unique thing about Speaker's Notes—as compared with a word processing document—is that they include pictures of the **slides** you're talking about. If you are giving a **presentation,** by the way, you'll probably want to use either Speaker's Notes or an **outline** as the document you "talk from."

To create Speaker's Notes, you use **Notes Pages** view.

Spell-checking Presentations You can use the Tools

 Spelling command and the Spelling tool to check the spelling of words in your slides. After you choose the command or the tool, PowerPoint displays the Spelling dialog box. Use it to control how PowerPoint spell-checks and what PowerPoint does when it finds a possible error.

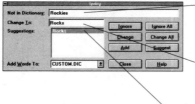

PowerPoint alerts you to words it can't find in its dictionary with the Not in Dictionary field.

PowerPoint suggests an alternative spelling in the Change To text box. But you can edit whatever PowerPoint suggests.

Other words that are spelled similarly to what you entered appear in the Suggestions list box. You can select any of these by clicking.

After PowerPoint finds a potentially misspelled word, you use the Spelling command buttons to indicate what PowerPoint should do:

Button	What it does
Ignore	Ignore only this occurrence of the word.
Ignore All	Ignore this and every other occurrence of the word in the presentation.
Change	Change this occurrence of the word to what the Change To text box shows.
Change All	Change this and every other occurrence of the word to what the Change To text box shows.
Add	Add the word to the spelling dictionary named in the Add Words To drop-down list box.
Suggest	Look through the PowerPoint spelling dictionary and the custom dictionary named in the Add Words To drop-down list box for similarly spelled words.

You can't spell-check words in OLE objects

When PowerPoint spell-checks the words in a presentation, it looks only at those words you've actually added with the PowerPoint application. It doesn't look at the words you've added in an OLE object with a supplementary application. As a result, you can't spell-check the words in a chart created with Graph, in an organization chart created with Microsoft Organization Chart, or objects created with other Microsoft Office applications: charts from Excel, for example, and tables from Word. To spell-check one of these other objects, you'll need to use the Spelling tool in the application that created the object.

Starting PowerPoint

You start a Windows-based **application** such as PowerPoint either manually after you've started Windows or as part of starting Windows.

Starting PowerPoint Manually

To start PowerPoint manually, follow these steps:

1 Start Windows by typing *win* at the MS-DOS prompt and pressing Enter.

2 Display the group in which PowerPoint is a program item. For example, if PowerPoint's group is Microsoft Office—and it probably is—choose the Window Microsoft Office command from the Program Manager menu bar.

3 Double-click the PowerPoint program item. PowerPoint displays the PowerPoint dialog box.

Starting a PowerPoint Presentation Automatically

Perhaps PowerPoint is your life. Perhaps you want to start PowerPoint each and every time you start Windows. If so, just follow these steps:

1 Start Windows—for example, by typing *win* at the MS-DOS prompt and pressing Enter.

2 Display the group in which PowerPoint is a program item. For example, if PowerPoint's group is Microsoft Office, choose the Window Microsoft Office command from the Program Manager menu bar.

3 Display the StartUp group—for example, by choosing the Window Startup command from the Program Manager menu bar.

4 Drag the PowerPoint application's program item icon from the group window—such as Microsoft Office—to the StartUp group window to move the program item. Or, if you just want to duplicate the program item, hold down Ctrl while you drag. (The next time you start Windows, Windows will start PowerPoint.)

After You've Started PowerPoint

After you or Windows has started PowerPoint, one of two things happens. If you haven't started PowerPoint before, PowerPoint asks if you want to see the Quick Preview tutorial. The Quick Preview tutorial describes PowerPoint and how you use it—all in general terms.

If you've started PowerPoint before or if you've finished the Quick Preview tutorial, PowerPoint displays a dialog box that asks how you want to get started.

S

If you don't know what to do next, use PowerPoint's **AutoContent Wizard** as an aid for building a presentation outline. (To do this, select the AutoContent Wizard option button and then choose OK.) Then, after you've built your outline, use the **Pick A Look Wizard** to spiff up your presentation.

Switching Tasks To **multitask,** or to run multiple applications simultaneously, in the Windows operating environment, you use the Control menu's Switch To command. Selecting this command displays the Task List dialog box, which works as described below.

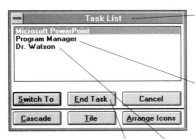

The Task List dialog box lists Program Manager as well as any other applications you (or Windows) have started.

To start a new application, double-click Program Manager. After Windows displays Program Manager, use it to start another application.

To switch to an application already running, double-click it. Or select it with the direction keys or the mouse and then choose Switch To.

Use the Cascade, Tile, and Arrange Icons command buttons to manage the application windows of the applications you've started.

You can use the End Task command button to stop a Windows-based application.

continues

Switching Tasks *(continued)*

Easy switching

You can cycle through the applications listed in the Task List dialog box using the keyboard. Press Alt+Tab to return to the last active application. Or hold down the Alt key and repeatedly press Tab to see message boxes that list the running applications, and release the Alt and Tab keys when the message box names the application you want to switch to. You can also press Alt+Esc to move through the open applications.

Switching Views ⁘ Views

Tables   PowerPoint lets you embed **Microsoft Word** tables as **OLE objects** in your **slides,** as long as you've also got Microsoft Word version 6.

For Microsoft Excel users

If you have Excel and know how to create simple worksheets, you don't need to embed Word tables. You can create an Excel worksheet and then move it to a PowerPoint presentation by dragging-and-dropping.

Adding a Table to an Existing Slide

To add a table to an existing slide, select the Insert Microsoft Word Table tool when you're in Slide view. After PowerPoint displays a drop-down list box, indicate the number of rows and columns you want in your table by dragging the mouse from the upper left square, or cell.

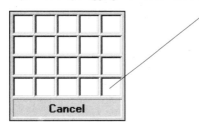

To add a table with four rows and five columns, drag the mouse from the upper left corner to the lower right corner.

After PowerPoint displays the Word table object in a separate window, fill in the table.

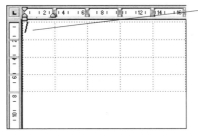

To fill in the table, simply click on the cells, or input blanks, and type whatever you want.

To return to the regular view of the presentation, click someplace outside the Word table object window.

continues

113

Tables *(continued)*

Adding a New Table Slide

To add a Word table to a new slide, you can follow these steps:

 1 Choose the Slide View button to display the Slide view of the presentation.

2 Display the slide you want the table slide to follow.

3 Choose the Insert New Slide command. PowerPoint displays the New Slide dialog box.

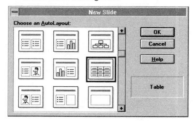

4 Select the slide layout that includes a table.

5 Choose OK. PowerPoint adds a new table slide to the presentation.

6 Entitle the table **slide title** by clicking the text **placeholder** labeled "Click to add title." Then type your title.

Creating a Table

To create a table from the table placeholder you added above, double-click the table object. PowerPoint displays the Insert Word Table dialog box.

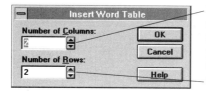

Tell Word how many columns you want. Don't worry about being too precise. It's easy to add columns (and rows) later on.

Tell Word how many rows you want, and then press Enter. Word inserts the table.

Logs	2000
Cedar Shakes	1000
Bricks	500
Total Costs	3500

To fill in the table, simply click the cells, or input blanks, and type whatever you want. I entered some data into the table cells.

A tip for spreadsheet users

You can use embedded Word tables like miniature spreadsheets. For example, you can enter formulas into cells that reference the values in other cells. To add a column of numbers, for example, select the table cell into which the total should go, choose the Insert Field command, and then enter *=sum(above)* into the Field Code text box. (I did this in the preceding figure to total my cabin construction costs.)

Formatting Embedded Word Tables

Tables you place in PowerPoint are actually Word tables you've embedded using **Object Linking and Embedding.** This means that after you double-click the Word **OLE object**, PowerPoint figures you want to change the embedded object. To do this, of course, you need access to the Word menu bar and its menus and commands. So that's what happens. Through the magic of Object Linking and Embedding, the menu bar and its menus change. In place of the PowerPoint menus and their commands, you have the Word menus and their commands. The Table menu commands let you change the appearance and structure of the table. The Format menu also provides commands to change the appearance of the text within the table.

continues

Tables *(continued)*

For quick table formatting

You can use the Table AutoFormat command, available when the Word table object is selected, to quickly format the selected table. When you choose this command, Word displays a dialog box that lists a bunch of predefined table formats and some check boxes you use to indicate whether Word should do anything special with the first or last row and column. Experiment with the options. Use the Preview box to see the effect.

Tabs   In the old days, you used the Tab key to move your type-writer carriage to the next tab stop. Typically, you did this for two reasons: to indent text—such as the first lines of paragraphs—and to create **tables.** In PowerPoint, para-graph indenting is a formatting choice. (This saves you from having to press Tab.) And tables are created using the Insert Table command.

Dare I say next what I'm thinking and what you're won-dering? I shall. Tabs are, for most PowerPoint users, ob-solete. There are better and easier ways to indent. There are better and easier ways to create tables.

Template A template is a **presentation** whose formatting you copy for another presentation. PowerPoint, by the way, comes with about 150 of these copyable presentations, or templates. So you can focus on the substance of your pre-sentation rather than having to worry about its form. Ap-pendix F in the *Microsoft PowerPoint User's Guide* provides color copies of the templates.

Template technical details

For those readers who need to know, let me be a bit more precise about just what a template is. A template includes an eight-color color scheme that will be used for a presentation. It includes a Slide Master that will describe any graphic objects you want plopped on each of the slides and the default text formatting the template uses. And it includes a set of AutoLayouts.

Selecting a Template with the Pick A Look Wizard

When you use the **Pick A Look Wizard,** one of the choices you indirectly make is which template you'll use as the design foundation for your presentation.

Selecting a Template Directly

You can also select a template directly. To apply a different presentation template to the open presentation, you use the Format Presentation Template command. Or you can choose the File New command or select the New tool and select the Current Presentation Format option button in the PowerPoint dialog box.

You can select a template and use it to specify the design of a brand-new presentation by starting PowerPoint and selecting the Template option button in the PowerPoint dialog box. Or, if PowerPoint is already running, you can select a template by choosing the File New command or by selecting the New tool and selecting the Template option button in the PowerPoint dialog box.

After you've indicated that you want to select a presentation template directly, PowerPoint displays the Presentation Template dialog box.

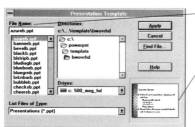

Use the File Name, Directories, and Drives boxes to locate and identify the template.

Click a template, and PowerPoint displays an example slide in the preview box.

continues

Template *(continued)*

Finding Templates

Templates are grouped into directories that correspond to the presentation medium you will use. Templates appropriate for **35mm slides** and on-screen presentations are stored in the SLDSHOW directory. Templates that work for black-and-white overheads are stored in the BWOVRHD directory. Templates that work for color overheads are stored in the CLROVRHD directory.

You can also use an existing presentation as a template. When you do, PowerPoint copies the existing presentation's design but not its content.

Color Schemes; Slide Masters

Text Box In this book, I've used the term *text box* to refer to the little snippets of text you add with the **Drawing** toolbar's Text tool. My use of the term is, admittedly, arbitrary. But I needed a way to differentiate the text you place into **text objects** and into the **outline** and the text you add with the Drawing toolbar. The reason is that text you add with the Drawing toolbar isn't part of the outline. Text you enter into text objects, in comparison, is part of the outline.

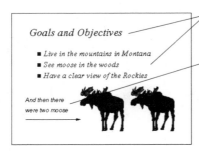

This is text object text, and it appears in the outline.

This is text box text, and it doesn't appear in the outline.

Text Object You'll need to add text objects to **slides** for their **slide titles.** In addition, you will almost always add lines of text, often as bulleted lists of points, to the slides in a **presentation.** You can add this title and bullet point text using either Outline view or Slide view.

Adding Text with Outline View

When you add text using Outline view, you type slide titles as the first outline level. You enter the major headings, or bullet points, as the second outline level. You enter the minor headings, or bullet points, within a major heading as the third outline level, and so on. You can enter as many as five levels in an outline—although I wish you luck in fitting in five legible levels on a slide.

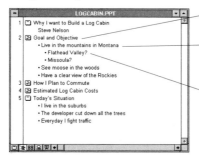

Enter slide titles as the first outline level.

Enter major headings, or bullet points, as the second outline level.

Enter minor headings, or bullet points within bullet points, as the third outline level.

By default, each line of text is a bullet point. It will start with a **bullet.** You can remove or change a bullet, however, by selecting the bullet point and choosing the Format Bullet command.

 If you enter a line of text into the wrong outline level, you can use the Outlining toolbar's Promote and Demote tools to move the line to the appropriate level. Something you've entered as a slide title, for example, can easily be moved to a major heading or major bullet point.

 If you enter a line of text in the wrong place, you can use the Outline toolbar's Move Up and Move Down tools.

continues

119

POWERPOINT A TO Z

Text Object *(continued)*

Adding Text with Slide View

When you add text using Slide view, you type text into **placeholders** for titles and bulleted list objects. These text placeholders display as rectangles with dashed line borders. Inside the rectangles, PowerPoint displays the instruction "Click to add title" or "Click to add text."

In a text placeholder, each line of text is a bullet point. To end a line of text and add a text placeholder for the next bullet point, press Enter. To end a line of text but not the bullet point, you can press shift+Enter.

You can remove or change the bullets. To do this, select the bullet point and choose the Format Bullet command.

If you enter a line of text into the wrong outline level—you enter a major bullet point as a minor bullet point, for example—select the bullet and drag it left or right. Drag left to promote the bullet point. Drag right to demote the bullet point.

If you enter a line of text in the wrong place—you enter the fourth bullet point as the third bullet point, say—select the bullet and drag it up or down.

Deleting Text

To delete text, position the **insertion point** by clicking or using the Left and Right direction keys. Use the Backspace key to erase the character preceding the insertion point; use the Del key to erase the character following the insertion point.

Replacing Text

To replace text, position the insertion point at the beginning of the text by clicking. Drag the mouse to the last character of the text. Then type the replacement text. What you type replaces the selected text.

Entering Characters That Aren't on the Keyboard

If you want to enter a character that doesn't show on the keyboard, you'll need to use an **ANSI character,** the Windows **Character Map,** or a Symbol or Dingbat **font** that provides kooky characters.

Copying and Moving Text Between Text Objects

To copy text from one text object to another, use the Edit Copy and Edit Paste commands or their toolbar counterparts: Copy and Paste. To move text from one text object to another, use the Edit Cut or Edit Paste commands or their toolbar counterparts: Cut and Paste.

Moving Text Objects and Placeholders

You can move a text object or an empty text object (placeholder) by selecting the object and dragging. Select a text object or a placeholder by clicking its border.

Resizing Text Objects and Placeholders

You can resize a text object or an empty text object (placeholder) by selecting it and then dragging its selection handles. Select a text object or a placeholder by clicking its border. Drag the corner selection handles to change both the height and width at the same time. Drag side selection handles to change only the height or width.

continues

Text Object *(continued)*

Anchoring Text in a Text Object

You can choose an anchor point for the text that sits inside the text object. (Normally, text is anchored to the top left corner of the text object box.) To change the anchor point, follow these steps:

1 Select the text object—such as by clicking.

2 Choose the Format Text Anchor command.

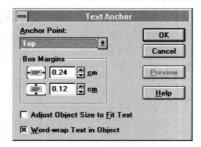

3 Activate the Anchor Point drop-down list box.

4 Select the point to which the text should be anchored: Top, Middle, or Bottom; or Top Centered, Middle Centered, or Bottom Centered.

5 Choose OK.

Setting Text Object Box Margins

You can also set text object box margins using the Text Anchor dialog box. To do this, follow these steps:

1 Select the text object—such as by clicking.

2 Choose the Format Text Anchor command. PowerPoint displays the Text Anchor dialog box.

3 Use the Box Margins boxes to specify the margin, or space, between the text and the edges of the text object box.

4 Choose OK.

A perfect fit

To shrink a text object box so that it just fits the text it holds, select the text object, choose the Format Text Anchor command, mark the Adjust Object Size to Fit Text check box, and choose OK.

Tip of the Day
After PowerPoint starts, it displays a message box with some helpful nugget of knowledge, called the Tip of the Day. You can choose OK to continue. You don't have to read the tip.

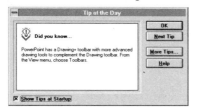

If you don't read the tip of the day
Unmark the Show Tips at Startup check box if you're not interested in reading the Tip of the Day.

Title Slide
The title slide is the first **slide** in a **presentation.** It probably names the presentation and the presenter. If you start creating a presentation with the **AutoContent Wizard,** it creates a title slide for you.

> **Slide Titles**

Toolbars
Toolbars are those rows of buttons and boxes that appear at the top of your window just below the menu bar. PowerPoint initially displays the Standard toolbar and the Formatting toolbar. But PowerPoint also provides several other toolbars. You can add and remove any toolbar by pointing to the toolbar, clicking the right mouse button (instead of the usual left button), and then—when PowerPoint displays a list of the available toolbars—selecting the one you want. (You can also use the View Toolbars command to accomplish the same thing.)

continues

Toolbars *(continued)*

Toolbar button names

If you place the mouse pointer on a toolbar button or box,
PowerPoint displays the tool name in a tiny yellow box. This tiny
yellow box is called a ToolTip.

Transition Initially, PowerPoint doesn't use any slide-to-slide
transition: One minute it shows your first slide, for example, and the next minute it shows your second slide.
You can use slide-to-slide transitions, however.

Specifying Slide-to-Slide Transitions

To specify slide-to-slide transitions, follow these steps:

 1 Choose the Slide Sorter View button.

2 Select the slide from which you want to transition. Or, to use the
transition for more than one slide, select all the slides for which
you want to specify a transition. (You can select multiple slides by
dragging the mouse from the upper left corner to the lower right
corner of a rectangle that encompasses the slides.)

3 Choose the Tools Transition command. PowerPoint displays the
Transition dialog box.

4 Select a transition from the Effect list box. PowerPoint uses the
preview box shown in the lower right corner of the dialog box to
demonstrate the effect.

5 Select a Speed setting if you don't like the default transition speed, Fast.

6 Use the Advance option buttons to specify what triggers transitions, a mouse click or the passage of time. (If you say that PowerPoint should automatically transition from this slide, you'll also need to specify the seconds that PowerPoint should display the slide.)

TrueType TrueType is Microsoft Corporation's scalable **font** technology. Using TrueType fonts in your presentations delivers several benefits. First, Windows and Microsoft Windows-based applications come with some cool TrueType fonts. (OK. Maybe that shouldn't count as a benefit, but you don't get any PostScript fonts with Windows or with Microsoft applications. PostScript is the competitive scalable font product.) Second, because of the way a scalable font is created, it's easy for Windows and Windows-based applications, such as PowerPoint, to change the **point** size in a way that results in legible fonts. Third, you can embed TrueType fonts in your presentations. Thus, you can show a presentation on different personal computers—and still have everything look right. Windows identifies TrueType fonts in the various Font list boxes with the **T** prefix.

Adding fonts

If you purchase additional TrueType fonts, you can add them using Control Panel's Settings Fonts command. To do this, you start the Control Panel application. It's probably located in the Main program group.

Underlined Characters

 You can <u>underline</u> characters by selecting them and then pressing Ctrl+U or selecting the Underline tool. You can also use the Format Font command.

Undo

 You can undo your most recent change to a **presentation**. Simply select the Undo tool. Or choose the Edit Undo command.

Unerasing Presentation Files

You should know that it might be possible to recover, or unerase, a presentation file. As long as you've got MS-DOS version 5 or later, you can unerase files. You might need to use the MS-DOS UNDELETE command. Or you might be able to use the Windows Undelete utility, which comes with MS-DOS versions 6 and later.

I'm not going to describe here how you do this. The mechanics relate to MS-DOS or Windows and not to PowerPoint. I did want to mention that unerasing is possible, however. If you've accidentally deleted the presentation you need for a meeting that starts in 15 minutes, you've got just about enough time to look up "Undelete" in the MS-DOS or Windows documentation and then follow the instructions given there for unerasing the presentation. I won't say anything more. You need to get started.

Vector Images

Vector images are usually produced by **drawing** programs. As compared with **bit map images**, they have the advantage that they consist of drawn **objects**—lines and shapes—that you can edit. (A bit map image consists of pixels of light that you have to recolor.) The **clip art** objects that come with PowerPoint, for example, are all vector images.

Video   Using the Windows Media Player accessory, you can create videos, or movies. Using **object linking and embedding,** you can insert one of these videos, or movies, into a
slide as an **OLE object.** When you're not running the
video or showing the movie, what you'll usually see on
the face of the slide is the first frame of the movie.

If you do insert a video OLE object into a **slide,** you can
show the movie by double-clicking the object icon, or
you can tell PowerPoint to show the movie automatically.

Viewer   Viewer is a separate **application** you can use to run
PowerPoint **presentations** on other people's computers.
Microsoft's PowerPoint licensing agreement, in fact, lets
you freely copy the Viewer application so that you can
easily and legally distribute PowerPoint presentations.

Installing Viewer on Another Computer
You'll need to find the PowerPoint disk labeled PowerPoint Viewer
Disk 11. After you've done this, follow these steps:

1 Insert Disk 11 into the
floppy drive of the
other computer.

2 Start or switch to the
Windows Program
Manager.

3 Choose the File Run
command.

4 Type *a:\vsetup* or
b:\vsetup into the text
box and press Enter.
(The *a:* or *b:* part
identifies the floppy
disk drive.)

5 Follow the on-screen
instructions. For ex-
ample, the Viewer
Setup program will ask
where it should install
Viewer.

continues

127

Viewer *(continued)*

Using Viewer

To use Viewer to run a slide-show presentation, you start the
PowerPoint Viewer application. You start PowerPoint Viewer the same
way you start PowerPoint: Display the program group window with the
PowerPoint Viewer icon, and double-click the icon.

After you start PowerPoint Viewer, it displays a dialog box that asks
for the presentation you want to show. Opening a presentation file
with PowerPoint Viewer works the same as opening a file with
PowerPoint. If you don't know or remember how to do this, refer to the
Opening Presentations or the **Slide Show** entry.

After you've started Viewer and opened a presentation, you run the
slide show in the usual way.

Copying Presentation Files

To copy files, you use the Windows File Manager application. To start
File Manager, display the Main group and double-click the File
Manager program item.

To copy a file to a floppy disk with the mouse, follow these steps:

1 Click the disk drive icon of the drive that contains the presentation
file.

2 Click the directory and, if necessary, double-click the subdirectory
that contains the presentation file.

3 Select the presentation file.

4 Drag the presentation file to the floppy disk drive icon.

V

Copying a Presentation File with the File Copy Command

To copy a presentation file to a floppy disk with the keyboard, follow these steps:

1 Choose the File Copy command.

2 Enter the file name and the path for the presentation you want to copy.

3 Enter the path for the location to which you want to copy the presentation—such as A: if you want to copy the file to drive A.

4 Choose OK.

About File Manager

You can do a lot more with File Manager than I've described here. If you have questions about how File Manager works or if you want to do something more sophisticated than I've described, refer to your Windows user documentation.

 **Switching Tasks**

Views   You can look at the information in a **presentation** in different ways: as the **slides,** or pages, in a presentation, as **outlines** that show the **slide titles** and any **text object** text, in **Slide Sorter** view that lets you arrange and rearrange the slides and their order, in **Notes Pages** view, which lets you see any **Speaker's Notes** you've created for a slide, and in **Slide Show** view, which shows the slides using your full screen.

continues

Views *(continued)*

Flip-Flopping Between Views

To change your view, choose the View menu command that names the view. Or use one of the View buttons as described in the table that follows. (The view buttons appear in the lower left corner of the presentation **document window.**)

Button	Which view it displays
▢	Slide view
☰	Outline view
▦	Slide Sorter view
▣	Notes Pages view
▤	Slide Show view

Wizards
PowerPoint provides two wizards. Each is enormously helpful in expediting the creation of a presentation. The **AutoContent Wizard** helps you organize your information. The **Pick A Look Wizard** helps you choose a **color scheme** and format for your information.

WordArt
PowerPoint comes with a supplementary **application,** called WordArt, that lets you manipulate text in all sorts of crazy ways. When you use WordArt, what you actually do is embed WordArt **OLE objects** into a presentation.

Starting WordArt

You start WordArt by telling PowerPoint you want to insert a WordArt OLE object into a **slide.** This operation works as described in the **Embedding New Objects** entry. For this reason, I won't repeat that discussion here. The only thing you need to do is select WordArt version 2 as the object application.

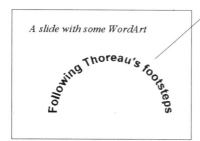

A slide with text that I've manipulated with WordArt.

Creating a WordArt Object

After you've started WordArt, you'll see the WordArt window.

Enter the text you want to manipulate.

continues

WordArt *(continued)*

Formatting the WordArt Object Text

You can use the Format menu commands or the Formatting toolbar buttons and boxes to manipulate the text you've entered. The toolbar buttons and boxes are probably the easiest and quickest way to manipulate the text. The table below describes them.

Tool	What it does
— Plain Text ⬇	The *Shape* tool selects a shape for the text: circular, arched, curved, and so on.
Arial ⬇	The *Font* tool selects a typeface for the text.
Best Fit ⬇	The *Size* tool selects a point size for the text or selects the Best Fit to tell WordArt it should size the text.
B	The *Bold* tool **boldfaces** the text.
I	The *Italic* tool *italicizes* the text.
Ee	The *Even Height* tool makes all the characters the same height.
◁	The *Flip* tool rotates the text so that it's on its side.
⋆Ȧ⋆	The *Stretch* tool expands the text so that it fills the WordArt object.
⸨≣	This will be a big surprise to you, no doubt. But get this. The *Align* tool aligns your text: left-align, right-align, center, and so on.
A̶V̶	The *Spacing Between Characters* tool adjusts the character kerning.
↺	The *Rotation* tool turns, or spins, the text.

Tool	What it does
▨	The *Shading* tool colors and selects a pattern for the text.
▣	The *Shadow* tool adds shadowing to the text.
▤	The *Border* tool draws a border line around the text.

Wordwrap

PowerPoint wordwraps the text you enter into a **text object** and a **text box.** In other words, it moves the **insertion point** to the next line after you run out of room on the current line. Because it wants to be helpful, PowerPoint will also move big words to the next line if the move makes things fit better. Wordwrap is a simple little feature. You'll almost certainly want to use it.

If for some crazy reason you don't want to use it, however, you can use the Format Text Anchor command to turn it off. To do this, select the text object or text box, choose the Format Text Anchor command, and unmark the Wordwrap Text in Object check box.

Zooming You can magnify and reduce, or shrink, the size of the
characters and the images shown in the **document
window.** You can use either the View Zoom command or
the Zoom Control tool. I'm not sure zooming deserves an
entry, by the way. It did seem to me, though, that since
this part is called A to Z, it should have at least one Z
entry.

Magnifying

Activate the Zoom Control drop-down box on the Standard toolbar or
choose the View Zoom command. Then select a percentage. Selecting
200%, for example, magnifies everything to twice its actual size.

Shrinking

Activate the Zoom Control drop-down list box on the Standard toolbar
or choose the View Zoom command. Then select a percentage.
Selecting 50%, for example, reduces everything to half its actual size.

Actual size might vary

When you zoom a presentation, you don't change the character or image size.
You merely magnify or shrink the display. As a result, zooming doesn't change the
appearance of your printed presentation.

TROUBLE-SHOOTING

••

Got a problem? Starting on the next page are solutions to the problems that plague new users of Microsoft PowerPoint. You'll be on your way— and safely out of danger—in no time.

DESIGN AND LAYOUT

Your Output Looks Ugly   If your output doesn't look good or it doesn't present well, you're probably using a **color scheme** that's incompatible with your output medium. Electronic slide shows and **35mm slides**, for example, look best with dark (but not black) backgrounds and light (but usually not white) text. Color overhead transparencies look best with light backgrounds and dark text. And black-and-white output—such as that you print on a laser printer—limits you to using black, white, and gray.

Use the Pick A Look Wizard

Although you can use the Format Slide Color Scheme command to individually select the **colors** in the eight-color color scheme, you'll find it easier to use the **Pick A Look Wizard** to select an appropriate color scheme. To do this, open the **presentation**, select the Pick A Look Wizard tool, and then, when the wizard displays the second dialog box, select the option button that corresponds to the output medium you'll use the next time you print or show the **slide show**.

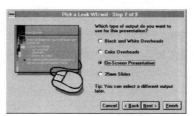

Select the option button that corresponds to your output medium.

When you can use the Pick A Look Wizard

You can use the Pick A Look Wizard any time you want to change the color scheme of a presentation. If you're printing color overhead transparencies and black-and-white audience handout pages, you would use the Pick A Look Wizard twice: once to select an appropriate color scheme for the color overheads and another time to select an appropriate black-and-white color scheme for the handout pages.

You Can't Fit Everything You Want on a Slide

You'll often find it challenging to fit all the information you want on a **slide.** You can, however, employ several techniques to fill slides with the appropriate volume of information.

Turn a slide into multiple slides

If you're got too much information to put on a slide, you might be trying to use one slide when you really need two (or more) slides. In this case, break up, or **chunkify,** the information.

You can easily turn one slide into more than one slide using **Outline** view. (Just promote main headings to **slide titles.**) You can move objects by using the Edit Cut and Edit Paste commands. You can copy objects by using the Edit Copy and Edit Paste commands.

If some of the information is less important—perhaps you're unsure viewers will need or want to see it—you might even want to place it on a **hidden slide.**

Use Speaker's Notes

Another reason your slides might be cluttered is that you're including too much information. You might be trying to fit information that shouldn't go on a slide. If you want to be sure that people receive the information, you can place the information in **Notes Pages.** This way you're sure to include the information in the verbal portion of your presentation—and communicate it that way—but it won't clutter a slide.

Use drill-down documents

If you've got an important supporting **document**—a **Microsoft Excel** worksheet, say—that you want to include in a presentation, you might not need to place the worksheet on a slide. It might make more sense to insert the worksheet in the presentation as a **drill-down document.** In this way, someone viewing the slide show on a computer can double-click, or drill-down on, the object to review the supporting information.

 Copying Data; Moving Data

Your Audience Includes Men with Defective Color Vision

Defective color vision, or color blindness, is common among men. In a group of men of European descent, for example, as many as 1 in 12 will have at least some trouble differentiating hues, or colors. (Defective color vision is less common among men of African or Asian descent and relatively uncommon among women.) Although this seems like a funny topic for a Field Guide, you'll want to take color blindness into account. Not doing so can be an obstacle to successful presentations.

Differentiate colors with luminance

One thing you can do to accommodate color blindness is to be sure you use colors with different **luminance.** This works because it allows someone who can't differentiate **hue** to differentiate luminance. PowerPoint's **color schemes** do this automatically, by the way, so you don't need to worry about luminance if you stick with the PowerPoint color schemes.

If you create your own color schemes, you can adjust the luminance of the individual colors by using the Format Slide Color Scheme command. To do this, take the following steps:

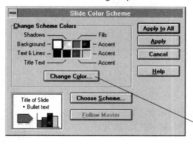

1 Choose the Format Slide Color Scheme command. PowerPoint displays the Slide Color Scheme dialog box.

2 Click the color for which you want to adjust luminance.

3 Choose the Change Color command button. PowerPoint displays a Colors dialog box that provides 90 colored buttons for you to choose from. (I have not included this dialog box here, but you could select a color by clicking one of its boxes.)

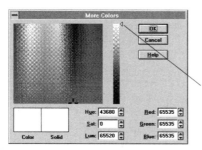

4 Choose the More Colors command button. PowerPoint displays the More Colors dialog box.

5 Drag this triangle up and down to change the color luminance. Or you can use the Lum box. (After you drag the luminance triangle and release the mouse button, PowerPoint adjusts the luminance setting.)

Avoid easily confused color combinations

Another thing you can do to accommodate color blindness is to shy away from color combinations that are easily confused. Red and green are the most commonly confused colors and are, therefore, a risky combination for a presentation. Even one about tiny reindeer and a fat man in a red suit.

PowerPoint's color schemes avoid red-green color combinations for this exact reason, by the way.

Traffic-light trivia

Here's an interesting bit of trivia regarding color blindness and traffic lights. The green light in a traffic light isn't really green. It's blue-green. The reason for this is that color-blind drivers who can't differentiate red from green hues can still differentiate a non-blue hue from a blue hue. OK. I know what you're thinking now. You're wondering, "Why can't they just identify the light by position?" Sorry, but I don't know. The guy who told me about traffic light hues is an ophthalmology professor at the University of Chicago and not a highway engineer.

FILES

You Can't Save a Presentation

PowerPoint needs a certain amount of special memory, called system resources memory, to save a **presentation**. If your system resources get too low, therefore, you can run into some pretty serious problems. Fortunately, as long as you keep your cool, this doesn't have to be a disaster. Your basic tack is a simple one. You want to free up system resources and then try resaving the presentation.

Close your other open applications

Switch to any of your other open **applications** and close them. You can switch to the other open applications by choosing the PowerPoint Control menu's Switch To command, selecting the other application from the Task List dialog box, and then choosing the End Task button.

After you've closed all the other applications (and saved their documents if that's appropriate), return to PowerPoint and try resaving the presentation you couldn't save earlier.

If you're the superstitious sort, go ahead and cross your fingers. It won't make any difference. But it might make you feel better.

Close your other open presentations

If you've opened more than one presentation, you might be able to free system resources memory by closing the other presentation. Of course, this might present its own problem if this other presentation also needs to be saved. In extreme cases, you might need to close the presentation that has the fewest unsaved changes without saving it.

 Saving Presentations; Switching Tasks

You Can't Find a Presentation

If you've got a large hard disk with hundreds of directories and thousands of files, it is embarrassingly easy to loose a presentation. Fortunately, PowerPoint provides a command that helps you find lost files.

Use the File Find File command

You can usually use the File Find File command to locate lost presentations. After you choose the command, PowerPoint displays the Find File dialog box (unless this is the first time you've used File Find File—see below).

On the left half of the dialog box, PowerPoint lists all presentation files on your disk. You can scroll through the list to find the presentation file you want.

PowerPoint shows a picture of the selected presentation's **title slide** if the View drop-down list shows Preview.

You can use choose other views too. The File Info view shows MS-DOS file information. The Summary view shows the information you enter into the Info Summary dialog box, which PowerPoint displays the first time you save a presentation.

After you find the presentation you want, choose Open.

continues

You Can't Find a Presentation *(continued)*

The first time you use File Find File

The first time—and only the first time—you (or someone else) uses the File Find File command, PowerPoint displays the Search dialog box. This dialog box lets you describe the criteria you want to use to search for document files, the disk you want to search, and the directories you want to search. If you see this other dialog box on your screen and not the one shown above, enter the File Name as *.ppt. Specify the location as your hard disk. Be sure the Include Subdirectories check box is marked. If you later want to change these search criteria, choose the Find File dialog box's Search command button.

 File Summary; Opening Presentations; Saving Presentations

PRINTING

Your Printer Stalls

Printing in color is slow. Printing graphics is slow. If you combine color and graphics, printing is really slow. This slowness, besides causing you irritation, can cause your printer problems. The Windows Print Manager, which does the actual printing, expects to be able to send your printer more data regularly (often every 45 seconds). If it takes three minutes to print a page, however, Print Manager can't send the printer more information and might conclude that your printer isn't responding. Shortly after reaching this conclusion, Print Manager will display an on-screen message saying something like, "That printer of yours isn't responding again, and I'm pretty much at my wits' end."

Tell Print Manager to retry

To tell Print Manager to start printing again, choose the Retry command button if it appears on the message box. This might be all you need to you do. Or, if there are still several pages left in the presentation, you might need to sit in front of your computer and choose Retry a few more times.

Increase the printer's transmission Retry setting

If you're frequently getting the "Printer isn't respond-ing" message or you're going to be doing a lot of pre-sentation printing, you might want to tell Print Manager it's OK that your printer isn't quite as quick as Print Manager would like it to be. To do this, take the follow-ing steps:

1 Start the Control Panel application. It's prob-ably located in the Main prgroup.

2 Choose the Settings Printers command, or double-click the Print-ers icon. Control Panel displays the Printers dialog box.

3 Select the printer you're having trouble with from the Installed Printers list box.

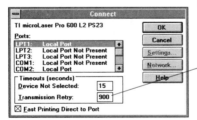

4 Choose the Connect command button. Con-trol Panel displays the Connect dialog box.

5 Set the Transmission Retry value to some-thing big. Something really big.

Setting the Transmission Retry value

The Transmission Retry value, in essence, tells Print Manager how long to wait for a printer before notifying you that the printer isn't responding. For non-PostScript printers, Windows assumes 45 seconds is long enough. For PostScript printers, Windows assumes 90 seconds is long enough. But, if you're printing graphics or you're printing in color, you can and should dramatically increase these settings. The 900 seconds setting shown here isn't a joke, sadly. It's the suggested setting for a color PostScript printer.

Your Printed Slides Are Too Black

If you're printing presentations on a regular black-ink-on-white-paper printer, you need to be sure that PowerPoint knows you're doing this. Otherwise, it'll lay down a page full of black ink or toner to create every color except white. When this happens, you get terrible looking handouts because almost everything is black and gray. (You also use a lot of ink or toner.)

Use the Black & White printing options

If you're only printing the presentation in black and white a single time, you can use the Black & White printing options. PowerPoint makes these available in the Print dialog box, which appears after you choose the File Print command.

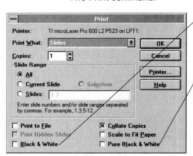

Mark the Black & White check box to convert colors to black and white and gray.

Mark the Pure Black & White check box to convert colors to black and white. (This option is faster than Black & White but is not as attractive.)

Tell the Pick A Look Wizard you're printing in black and white

If you'll almost always show the presentation in black and white, you can change the color scheme to one that uses black, white, and several shades of gray. To do this, follow these steps:

1 Open the presentation.

2 Select the Pick A Look Wizard tool to start the Pick A Look Wizard.

3 Select the Black and White Overheads option button when the wizard displays the second dialog box.

4 After you indicate you want a black-and-white color scheme, choose Finish to skip the rest of the wizard's steps.

Remove background visual elements

You might also want to remove the Slide Master's background visual elements if these clutter and darken the printed pages of a presentation. You can do this by taking the following steps:

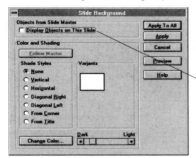

1 Choose the Format Slide Background command. PowerPoint displays the Slide Background dialog box.

2 Unmark the Display Objects on This Slide check box.

3 Choose the Apply command button to remove the Slide Master's background visual elements from the current slide. Or choose the Apply to All command button to remove the Slide Master's background visual elements from all the slides.

 Slide Master

True confession

In this book, the figures show slides using a black-and-white color scheme to minimize their blackness and grayness and a peculiar effect of color-figure to black-and-white-figure conversion called dithering. The figures also show slides without the Slide Master's background visual elements for the same reason. To be honest, this makes the slides less interesting. But it was necessary for legibility.

You Want to Cancel a Printing Presentation

If you've told PowerPoint to print a **presentation** you later realize you don't want to print, you might want to cancel the printing. This is particularly true if the document is long and you're using a slow printer—such as a color printer.

Cancel the printing from within PowerPoint

If PowerPoint shows a message box on your screen that says something along the lines of "Printing Slides," you can cancel the printing by pressing Esc or by choosing the message box's Cancel command button.

Switch to Print Manager and delete the job

When PowerPoint prints a presentation, it creates a print spool file that it sends to the Windows Print Manager. Print Manager then prints this print spool file as well as any other spool files that PowerPoint and other applications have sent.

To cancel the printing of a PowerPoint presentation after it's been sent to Print Manager, you need to follow these steps:

1 Choose the PowerPoint Control menu's Switch To command—for example, by pressing Ctrl+Esc.

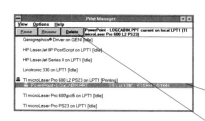

2 Select the Print Manager application from the task list—for example, by double-clicking.

3 Select the printing PowerPoint document.

4 Choose Print Manager's Delete command button.

5 After Print Manager asks if you want to cancel the printing document, choose OK.

 Control-Menu Commands; Printing Presentations; Switching Tasks

WINDOWS AND APPLICATIONS

You Want to Show a Presentation on Another Computer

You aren't limited to showing PowerPoint **presentations** on computers that have the PowerPoint **application**.

Install the PowerPoint Viewer

PowerPoint comes with another application, called **Viewer,** that lets you show PowerPoint presentations on other computers. The PowerPoint license agreement allows you to freely copy the Viewer application **file** and distribute it with your PowerPoint presentations. This means that you can show a presentation on another computer simply by copying the Viewer and presentation files.

You Can't Get an Application— such as PowerPoint— to Respond

It's unlikely but still possible that a bug in PowerPoint or a bug in some other program will cause an application to stop responding. If this happens, you won't be able to choose menu commands. And you might not be able to move the mouse pointer.

Terminate the unresponsive application

Unfortunately, if an application truly is unresponsive— if it ignores your keyboard and mouse actions—there's nothing you can do to make it start responding again. When this is the case, however, you can press Ctrl+Alt+Del.

Ctrl+Alt+Del—you press the three keys simultaneously—tells Windows to look at the active application and check for responsiveness. Windows makes this check and displays a message that tells you whether the application is, in fact, unresponsive.

```
This Windows application has stopped responding to the system.

*  Press ESC to cancel and return to Windows.
*  Press ENTER to close this application that is not responding.
*  You will lose any unsaved information in this application.
*  Press CTRL+ALT+DELETE to restart your computer. You will
   lose any unsaved information in all applications.

      Press ENTER for OK or ESC to cancel: OK
```

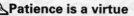

As the message text indicates, you can simply press Enter to close the unresponsive application. By the way, if the application isn't unresponsive, Windows knows this, and the message text indicates as much. In this case, you can press Enter to return to the application.

Patience is a virtue

Before you conclude that PowerPoint or some other application is ignoring you, consider the possibility that it is busy instead. PowerPoint, for example, might be redrawing a complicated slide. Other applications might be printing to a spool file (which gets sent to Print Manager for printing) or might be executing some command you've given.

You Get an Application Error

Sometimes an application asks Windows to do the impossible. When this happens—which isn't very often since the advent of Windows version 3.1, thankfully—Windows displays a message box that says there's been an application error.

Close the application

When Windows does alert you to an application error, it usually gives you two choices. You can close the application, or you can ignore the error.

If you've been working with a **presentation** and have made changes that you haven't yet saved, you can ignore the application error and then save the presentation. Save the presentation using a new file name, however. You don't want to replace the previous presentation file with a new corrupted presentation file. Then close the PowerPoint application.

If you haven't made any changes or haven't made changes you need to save, simply close the application.

 Saving Presentations

QUICK REFERENCE

Any time you explore some exotic location, you're bound to see flora and fauna you can't identify. To make sure you can identify the commands and toolbar buttons you see in Microsoft PowerPoint, the Quick Reference describes these items in systematic detail.

POWERPOINT MENU GUIDE

File Menu

New	Opens a new, blank presentation. Also gives you the option of starting a wizard or of copying the design of another presentation to help create the new presentation.
Open...	Retrieves an existing presentation from disk
Close	Removes the window of the active presentation from the screen
Save	Resaves the active presentation as long as you've saved it once before
Save As...	Saves a presentation the first time
Find File...	Looks for presentation files matching a specified description
Summary Info...	Displays information about the active presentation
Slide Setup...	Describes slides, or the layout of printed presentation pages
Print...	Prints the active presentation or some part of the active presentation
Exit	Closes, or stops, the Microsoft PowerPoint application

About the numbered File menu commands

PowerPoint also lists as File menu commands the last four presentations you saved. You can open a listed presentation by selecting it from the File menu.

Edit Menu

Undo	Reverses, or undoes, the last presentation change
Cut	Moves the current presentation selection to the Clipboard .
Copy	Moves a copy of the current presentation selection to the Clipboard
Paste	Moves the Clipboard contents to the active presentation
Paste Special...	Moves some portion of the Clipboard contents to the active presentation
Clear	Erases the current presentation selection
Select All	Selects everything in the presentation view's document window
Duplicate	Creates a duplicate copy of the current presentation selection
Delete Slide	Removes the selected slide from the presentation
Find...	Looks for text matching a specified description
Replace...	Looks for text matching a specified description and, optionally, replaces text
Links...	Describes, updates, and changes the selected object's link
Edit Object	Changes a selected object in some way. (Command name changes depending on the object and on the part of the object you've selected.)

View Menu

Slides	Displays a presentation one slide at a time
Outline	Displays presentation text in an outline, with slide titles being the highest outline level
Slide Sorter	Displays thumbnail sketches of slides on an on-screen light table
Notes Pages	Displays presentations one slide at a time but with space to enter Speaker's Notes (so you don't forget what you're going to say)
Slide Show...	Starts an on-screen slide show
Master	Displays the Master submenu

	Slide Master	Displays the Slide Master so that you can change all the slides in a presentation
	Outline Master	Displays the Outline Master so that you can change all the outline pages in a presentation
	Handout Master	Displays the Handout Master so that you can change all the handout pages in a presentation
	Notes Master	Displays the Notes Master so that you can change all the Notes Pages in a presentation

Toolbars...	Adds, removes, and customizes toolbars
Ruler	Adds and removes horizontal and vertical rulers in Slide view for easier object positioning
Guides	Adds and removes horizontal and vertical guidelines in Slide view for easier object positioning
Zoom...	Magnifies the presentation window by some specified percentage

Insert Menu

New Slide	Adds a new slide following the current slide
Date	Adds the date to the active presentation's Slide Master. (Date will appear on all slides.)
Time	Adds the time to the active presentation's Slide Master. (Time will appear on all slides.)
Page Number	Adds the page number to the active presentation's Slide Master. (Page number will appear on all slides.)
Slides From File...	Adds another presentation's slides to the current presentation
Slides From Outline...	Adds slides to the current presentation by importing an outline
Clip Art...	Lets you add an image from the Microsoft ClipArt Gallery to the slide
Picture...	Adds a graphic image, or picture, to the slide
Microsoft Word Table...	Adds a Word table object to the slide as long you have Word version 6
Microsoft Graph...	Adds a graph object to the slide
Object...	Adds an embedded or a linked object to a slide in the active presentation

Format Menu

Font...	Changes selected text's font, style, and point size as well as some other stuff too specific to mention here
Bullet...	Changes and removes bullets from the selected bulleted list
Alignment	Displays the Alignment submenu

Left	Left-aligns selected text
Center	Centers selected text
Right	Right-aligns selected text
Justify	Right- and left-justifies selected text

Line **S**pacing...	Changes between-the-lines spacing within and between paragraphs
Change Cas**e**...	Changes case (upper vs. lower) of selected text
Pe**r**iods...	Adds and removes periods from the ends of selected paragraphs
Text Anchor...	Specifies how text connects and wordwraps inside a text object or text box
Colors And **L**ines...	Changes colors of selected objects and lines and weights and styles of selected lines
S**h**adow...	Adds and removes shadowing from the selected object
Pic**k** Up Style	Copies the selected text or selected object formatting so that you can apply it somewhere else. (Command name changes depending on what is selected.)
Apply **S**tyle	Applies the text or object formatting you've already copied, or picked up, to the selected text or selected object. (Command name changes depending on what was selected.)
Presentation Template...	Lets you apply the design of a presentation template or of an existing presentation to the active presentation

Pick A Look Wizard...	Starts the Pick A Look Wizard
Slide Layout...	Changes a slide's AutoLayout
Slide Background...	Changes a slide's background, including any background artwork and its coloring
Slide Color Scheme...	Changes a slide's eight-color color scheme

Tools Menu

Spelling...	Checks the spelling of words in the active presentation but not of words in OLE objects embedded in the active presentation
Replace Fonts...	Makes font substitutions, such as Times Roman out and Arial in, throughout a presentation
Transition...	Specifies special effects for slide-to-slide transitions
Build...	Specifies special effects for incremental addition of bulleted list points in a slide
Hide Slide	Hides the selected slide so that it doesn't appear during a presentation
Play Settings...	Specifies how to show an OLE video object or how to play an OLE sound object
Recolor...	Changes the colors in the selected object
Crop Picture	Crops selected bit map image or vector image so that only a portion of the picture shows
Customize...	Lets you customize a PowerPoint toolbar
Options...	Changes PowerPoint's operation and appearance

Draw Menu

Group	Combines all selected objects into a single object for purposes of formatting and repositioning
Ungroup	Ungroups previously grouped objects
Regroup	Groups objects you've just ungrouped
Bring To Front	Repositions the selected object so that it appears above, or in front of, all other objects
Send To Back	Repositions the selected object so that it appears below, or in back of, all other objects
Bring Forward	Moves the selected object forward one position in a stack of objects
Send Backward	Moves the selected object backward one position in a stack of objects
Align	Displays the Align submenu

Lefts	Aligns the left edge of selected objects
Centers	Aligns the center points (between the left and right edges) of selected objects
Rights	Aligns the right edge of selected objects
Tops	Aligns the top edge of selected objects
Middles	Aligns the middle point (between the top and bottom edges) of selected objects
Bottoms	Aligns the bottom edge of selected objects

Snap To Grid	Aligns object edges to guidelines when the two items get close

158

Rotate/Flip	Displays the Rotate/Flip submenu

Free Rotate	Lets you rotate the selected object by dragging its corner selection handles
Rotate Left	First rotates the selected object 90 degrees counterclockwise and then lets you rotate the selected object by dragging its corner selection handles
Rotate Right	First rotates the selected object 90 degrees clockwise and then lets you rotate the selected object by dragging its corner selection handles
Flip Horizontal	Flips the selected object horizontally so that the new object image mirrors the old object image
Flip Vertical	Flips the selected object vertically so that the new object image mirrors the old object image
Flip Wilson	Not a submenu command, but the name of a comedian. Wilson hosted his own TV variety show during the 1970s.

Scale...	Changes the size of the selected object
Change AutoShape	Changes the shape of the selected object

Window Menu

Arrange All	Rearranges the open presentation's document windows so that they can all be seen
Fit To Page	Resizes a document window so that it fits the slide
Cascade	Rearranges the open presentation's document windows in a stack so that their title bars can all be seen

continues

159

Window Menu *(continued)*

About the numbered Window menu commands

PowerPoint also lists all the open presentations as numbered Window
menu commands. You can activate a listed presentation by choosing it
from the Window menu.

Help Menu

Contents	Displays a list of major Help topic categories
Search For Help On...	Provides help on a topic you select
Index	Displays a list of Help topics
Quick Preview	Starts the online tutorial, Welcome to Microsoft PowerPoint
Ti**p** Of The Day...	Displays the PowerPointTip of the Day
Cue Cards	Turns on Microsoft PowerPoint Cue Cards, which step you through creating presentations
Technical Support	Tells about support available for Microsoft PowerPoint
About Microsoft PowerPoint...	Displays the copyright notice, the software version number, and your computer's available memory

STANDARD TOOLBAR BUTTONS

Displays the New Presentation dialog box so that
you can start creating a new presentation

Displays the Open dialog box so that you can
retrieve an existing presentation

Saves the active presentation on disk

Prints the active presentation's slides

Checks the spelling of words in the active presentation

Moves the current presentation selection to the Clipboard

Moves a copy of the current presentation selection to the Clipboard

Moves the Clipboard contents to the active presentation

Copies formatting of the selected object so that you can apply it to another object

Undoes the last presentation change

Inserts a new slide following the current slide

Adds a Microsoft Word table to the slide

Adds a Microsoft Excel worksheet to the slide

Adds a graph to the slide

Adds an organization chart to the slide

Adds a clip art image to the slide

Starts the Pick A Look Wizard

Exports the presentation outline to Microsoft Word

Magnifies or reduces presentation contents by specified zoom percentage

Displays Help information about whatever you next click: a command, a piece of a presentation, or some element of the application or document window. Very handy.

FORMATTING TOOLBAR BUTTONS

Arial ⬇	Changes the selected text font or the presentation default font
24 ⬇	Changes the character point size of selected text or the presentation default point size
A	Increases the size of selected text to the next larger point size
A	Decreases the size of selected text to the next smaller point size
B	**Boldfaces** the characters in selected text
I	*Italicizes* the characters in selected text
<u>U</u>	<u>Underlines</u> the characters in selected text
S	Adds shadowing to selected text
A	Colors the characters of selected text
≣	Left-aligns selected text
≣	Centers selected text
☰	Adds and removes bullets from selected bulleted list
⬅	Promotes selected text to the next higher outline level
➡	Demotes selected text to the next lower outline level

GRAPH MENU GUIDE

File Menu

The File menu commands available when the selected object is a graph are the same as those available when the selected object isn't a graph. See the earlier listing of PowerPoint File menu commands.

Edit Menu

The Edit menu commands available when the selected object is a graph are basically a subset of the same commands available when the selected object isn't a graph. See the earlier listing of PowerPoint Edit menu commands.

View Menu

Datasheet	Turns off and on the display of the datasheet table providing the charted values. (Command is checked if the datasheet is displayed.)
Toolbars...	Adds, removes, and customizes toolbars
Zoom...	Magnifies the presentation window by some specified percentage

Insert Menu

Cells...	Adds a row, a column, or cells to the datasheet
Titles...	Adds titles to a chart and chart axes
Data Labels...	Adds text that describes plotted data points
Legend	Adds and removes legends
Axes...	Adds and removes horizontal and vertical axes
Gridlines...	Adds and removes horizontal and vertical gridlines
Trendline...	Plots a trend or regression line for selected data series
Error Bars...	Plots error bars for selected data series

Format Menu

Selected Object... — Changes the appearance of a selected data series or a chart object. This command name changes to reflect the selection.

Font... — Changes the selected text's font, style, and point size as well as some other stuff too specific to mention here

Number... — Changes the number formatting of the selected datasheet cells

Object Placement — Displays the Object Placement submenu

Bring To Front	Repositions the selected object so that it appears above, or in front of, all other objects
Send To Back	Repositions the selected object so that it appears below, or in back of, all other objects
Group	Combines all selected objects into a single object for purposes of formatting and repositioning

Column Width... — Changes the width of the selected column in a datasheet

Chart Type... — Selects one of the 14 chart types

AutoFormat... — Selects one of the preformatted versions available for the chart's type

3-D View... — Adjusts a 3-dimensional chart's elevation, rotation, or height

About the Graph Format menu

The Graph Format menu also includes numbered commands for each type of data marker used in the selected chart. You can format a data marker by choosing the marker's numbered command.

Tools Menu

Options...   Changes Graph's operation and appearance

Window Menu

The Window menu commands available in Graph are the same as those available in PowerPoint. See the earlier listing of PowerPoint Window menu commands.

Help Menu

The Help menu commands available when the selected object is a graph are a subset of the same commands available when the selected object isn't a graph. See the earlier listing of PowerPoint Help menu commands.

GRAPH TOOLBAR BUTTONS

🗐	Imports data from another document and plops it into a Graph datasheet
🗐	Imports a Microsoft Excel chart
🎴	Hides and removes the datasheet
✂	Moves the current chart selection to the Clipboard
🗐	Moves a copy of the current chart selection to the Clipboard
📋	Moves the Clipboard contents to the active chart
↶	Undoes the last chart change
🗐	Tells Graph you've arranged the data series by row
🎴	Tells Graph you've arranged the data series by column

continues

Activates a drop-down list of buttons showing the available chart types. Click a chart type's button to change to that chart type.

 Adds and removes major vertical axis gridlines

 Adds and removes major horizontal axis gridlines

 Adds and removes the legend

 Adds a text box to a chart

 Activates a drop-down list of buttons showing drawn objects. Click a drawn object's button to draw the object.

 Colors the selected object in a chart

 Adds a background pattern to the selected object in a chart

 Displays Help information about whatever you next click

SPECIAL CHARACTERS

3-D charts 60
35mm slides 9, 12, 105

A

active presentation 13
active window 12-13
aligning text 14
anchoring text 122
annotating slides 14
ANSI characters 14-15, 121
Apple File Exchange 15
Apple Macintosh 15
application errors 149
applications
    closing 36, 140, 149
    copying data between 37, 41,
      100-101
    defined 16
    moving data between 41,
      73-74, 100-101
    multitasking............................. 74
    sharing data between 6-7,
      100-101
    supplementary to PowerPoint .. 16
    troubleshooting 148-49
    unresponsive................... 148-49
application windows
    active 12-13
    Control-menu commands ... 35-36
    defined 16
    illustrated 2-3
    switching between 36, 111-12
arcs, drawing 43
Arc tool 43
area charts 59, 60
Arrowheads tool 45
ASCII characters 14
audience handouts 8, 9, 65

AutoContent Wizard
    defined 4, 5, 16
    running 17-18
    starting 17
AutoContent Wizard dialog
    boxes 17-18
AutoLayouts
    choosing 19
    defined 19
    list of 19-21
AutoShapes tool 43
axes, chart 62
Axes dialog box 62

B

Background Color dialog box 103
backgrounds 22, 32, 34, 103
Backspace key 40
bar charts 59, 60
bit map images 22
black & white printing 144, 145
boilerplate. See AutoLayouts; wizards
bold characters 22
Bold tool 22
borders, for drawn objects 44
branching 23
Bring Forward tool 45
Build dialog box 23
build slides 23
Build tool 23
Bullet dialog box 24
Bullet On/Off tool 24
bullets
    on build slides......................... 23
    removing................................. 24
    replacing 24

C

canceling printing 146-47
capitalization. *See* case, changing
case, changing 25
centering text 14
Change Case dialog box 25
Character Map application 25-26
characters
    spacing of 26
    special 14-15, 25-26, 121
charts. *See also* organization charts
    3-D 60
    adding slides for 56-57
    area 59, 60
    axes on 62
    bar 59, 60
    changing 63
    column 59, 60
    data categories for 63
    data labels on 61
    data markers for 63
    data series for 64
    doughnut 59
    formatting 62
    gridlines on 62
    legends on 58, 61
    line 59, 60
    moving 73-74
    pie 59, 60
    radar 59
    scatter 60
    surface 60
    titles on 61
    types of 58-60
    xy 60
Choose Scheme dialog box 34
chunkifying 27, 137
    See also outlines
circles, drawing 43

clip art. *See also* image formats
    adding to slides 28
    copying 29
    defined 27
    moving 29
    recoloring 29
    resizing 28
    ungrouping 29
ClipArt Gallery dialog box 28
Clipboard 30, 37, 73-74, 100
Close command 30, 36
closing
    applications 36, 140, 149
    presentations 30-31, 140
    windows 36
color, using 31, 67, 71, 98
color blindness 138-39
Color dialog box 33
coloring. *See also* recoloring
    clip art 44
    formatted objects 77
    lines 44
    text 31
Colors and Lines dialog box 77
color schemes
    built-in 32
    changing 34
    changing single colors 32-33,
        71, 98
    saving changes 34
    troubleshooting 136
column charts 59, 60
commands
    Control menu 35-36
    for Graph menus 163-65
    for PowerPoint menus 152-60
    shortcut menus 101
compound documents 78, 79
Control-menu commands 35-36
Copy command 30, 37,
    79, 91, 100

copying
  clip art 29
  data between applications 37,
    41, 100-101
  data within applications ... 37, 41
  formatting 38
  objects 37, 41, 100-101
  pictures 91
  presentation files 128-29
  slides between presentations .. 107
  text 37, 121
  using Clipboard 37, 100
  using drag-and-drop 41, 101
Copy tool 37, 91
corporate logos 71
Ctrl+Alt+Del 148-49
Cue Cards 39
cursor. See insertion point;
    selection cursor
Cut command 30, 73

Dashed Lines tool 45
data categories 63
data labels 61
Data Labels dialog box 61
data markers 63
data series 64
Datasheet window 57
dates, adding to slides 104
defective color vision 138-39
Delete command (File menu) ... 51
Delete Slide command
    (Edit menu) 40
deleting. See also unerasing pre-
    sentation files
  chart legends 61
  data 40
  objects 40
  pictures 91
  presentations 50-51
  text 40, 120

Del key 40
documents. See also presentations
  compound 78, 79
  defined 40
  drill-down 23, 47, 137
  importing 68-69
document windows
  active 12-13
  Control-menu commands ... 35-36
  defined 2, 3, 40
  switching between 13
doughnut charts 59
drag-and-drop 6, 41, 101, 107
dragging, defined 41
drawing. See also drawn objects
  arcs 43
  circles 43
  ellipses 43
  freeform shapes 43
  lines 42
  rectangles 43
  squares 43
  text boxes 42
  tools for 42-47
Drawing toolbar 42
Drawing+ toolbar 42
Draw menu 158-59
drawn objects. See also pictures
  borders for 44
  coloring 44
  creating 42-45
  flipping 47
  grouping 46
  moving 45
  resizing 46
  rotating 46
  selecting 41
  ungrouping 46
Draw Scale command 46, 78, 91
Draw Snap To Grid command 64
Draw Ungroup command 29
drill-down documents 23, 47, 137

E

Edit Clear command 40
Edit Copy command 30, 37, 79, 91, 100
Edit Cut command 30, 73
Edit Delete Slide command 40
Edit Find command 54
editing, in-place 7, 69
editing text 48
Edit menu (Graph) 163
Edit menu (PowerPoint) 153
Edit Paste command 30, 37, 73, 79, 91, 100
Edit Paste Special command 30, 79, 100, 101
Edit Replace command 96, 97
Edit Undo command 126
electronic slide shows
    defined 8, 9
    looping 71
    play list 92
    rehearsing 95
    running with PowerPoint 106
    running with Viewer 9, 106-7
elevators 48
ellipses, drawing 43
Ellipse tool 43
embedding. See also OLE objects
    of existing objects 49
    vs. linking 79, 101
    of new objects 50
ending lines of text 50
End key 75
erasing. See deleting
Excel 56, 72, 112, 137
exiting PowerPoint 51
exporting
    outlines 51-52
    slides 51
    text 51-52

F

File Copy command 129
File Delete command 51
File Find File command ... 141, 142
File Manager 128-29
File menu (Graph) 163
File menu (PowerPoint) 152
file names 52, 98
File New command 17, 117
File Open command 80
File Print command 94
File Run command 127
files. See also documents; presentations
    copying 128-29
    defined 52
    troubleshooting 140-42
File Save As command ... 51, 52, 98
File Save command.............. 98, 99
File Slide Setup command 105
file summaries 53
Fill Color tool 44
Fill On/Off tool 44
film recorders............................. 12
Find dialog box 54
Find File dialog box 141
finding text................................... 54
Flip Horizontal tool..................... 47
flipping drawn objects 47
Flip Vertical tool 47
Font dialog box 55
fonts
    bold 22
    changing from Formatting toolbar 54
    changing with Format Font command 55
    italic... 70
    replacing 96
    TrueType 125
    underline 126

Format Apply Object Style
  command 38
Format Apply Text Style
  command 38
Format Bullet command 24
Format Change Case
  command 25
Format Chart command 59
Format Chart Type
  command 58
Format Colors and Lines
  command 77
Format Font command 22, 31,
  55, 70, 103, 126
Format Line Spacing
  command 70
Format menu (Graph) 164
Format menu (PowerPoint) ....
  156-57
Format Painter tool 38
Format Periods command 86
Format Pick Up Object Style
  command 38
Format Pick Up Text Style
  command 38
Format Presentation Template
  command 117
Format Shadow command 77
Format Slide Background
  command 103, 145
Format Slide Color Scheme
  command 32, 34, 71, 98
Format Text Anchor command ... 122
formatting
  charts 62
  copying of 38
  objects 55, 77-78
  tables 115-16
  text 38, 103
Formatting toolbar 123, 162
freeform shapes, drawing 43
Freeform shape tool 43
Free Rotate tool 46

G

Graph application 56-63
  See also charts
graphic image formats 22, 126
  See also clip art; pictures
graphs. *See* charts
Graph toolbar 165
grid. *See* Snap To Grid command
gridlines, chart 62
Gridlines dialog box 62
grouping drawn objects 46
Group tool 46
guides 64

H

handouts 8, 9, 65
help feature 65
Help menu (Graph) 165
Help menu (PowerPoint) 65, 160
Help tool 66
hidden slides 66-67
Home key 75
hue 67

I

image formats 22, 126
  See also clip art; pictures
importing
  documents 68-69
  outlines 68, 82, 83
  slides 68
inactive windows 12
in-place editing 7, 69
Insert Axes command 62
Insert Clip Art command 28
Insert Clip Art tool 28
Insert Data Labels command 61

Insert Date command 104
Insert Field command 115
Insert Gridlines command 62
insertion point 70
Insert menu (Graph) 163
Insert menu (PowerPoint) 155
Insert Microsoft Word Table
    tool 113
Insert New Slide command 19,
    80, 114
Insert New Slide tool 19
Insert Object command 49, 50, 79
Insert Object dialog box 49, 50
Insert Page Number command 104
Insert Picture dialog box 90
Insert Time command 104
Insert Titles command 61
Insert Word Table dialog box 115
Ins key 85
italic characters 70
Italic tool 70

J

justifying text 14

K

kerning 26
keys, navigation 75

L

labels. *See* data labels
left aligning text 14
legends, chart
    adding 61
    moving 58
    removing 61
line charts 59, 60

Line Color tool 44
Line On/Off tool 44
lines
    as borders 44
    coloring 44
    dashed 45
    drawing 42
    spacing of 70
    text, ending 50
    thickness of 45
Line Spacing dialog box 70
Line Style tool 45
Line tool 42
linking. *See also* OLE objects
    vs. embedding 79, 101
    of existing objects 49
logos 71
looping slide shows 71
lowercase 25
luminance 71, 138-39

M

Macintosh 15
Maximize command 36
Media Player accessory 127
memory 72, 140
menu bar 2
menus
    Control menu, list of
        commands 35-36
    for Graph, list of
        commands 163-65
    for PowerPoint, list of
        commands 152-60
    shortcut-type 101
metafiles 51
Microsoft ClipArt Gallery dialog
    box 28
Microsoft Excel 56, 72, 112, 137
Microsoft Mail 72
Microsoft Office........................... 72

Microsoft PowerPoint Viewer
    dialog box 106
Microsoft Windows 3, 148-49
Microsoft Word 73, 82, 112-16
Minimize command 35
mouse pointers 93
Move command 35
moving
    chart legends 58
    charts 73-74
    clip art 29
    data between applications..... 41,
        73-74, 100-101
    data within applications ... 41, 73
    drawn objects 45
    pictures 91
    slides between presentations .. 107
    slides in Outline view 85
    slides to Clipboard 74
    text 73, 121
    text objects 121
    using Clipboard 73-74, 100
    using drag-and-drop 41, 73,
        74, 101
    windows 35
multitasking 74

N

naming presentations 52, 98
navigation keys 75
New Slide dialog box 19, 56,
    80, 114
New tool 17, 117
Next command 36
Notes Pages view 76, 130
Notes Pages View button ... 76, 130

O

object linking and embedding
    (OLE) 78-79
objects. *See also* drawn objects;
    OLE objects; text objects
    clip art as 27-29
    coloring 44, 77
    copying 37, 41, 100-101
    copying formatting 38
    defined 5, 76
    deleting 40
    formatting 55, 77-78
    moving 41, 73-74, 100-101
    resizing 46, 78, 91
    ungrouping 46, 104
    WordArt 130-33
OLE objects
    and branching 23
    defined 76, 78-79
    in-place editing 7, 69
    organization charts as 80-81
    selecting 99
    tables as 115-16
online help 65
Open dialog box 80
opening presentations 80
organization charts 80-81
outlines
    creating in PowerPoint 83-84
    creating in word processor 82-83
    importing 68, 82, 83
    moving slides in 85
    tools for creating 4, 84
    using to chunkify 137
Outline view 4-5, 82-85, 130
Outline View button 82, 130
overtyping 85

P

page numbers, adding to slides .. 104
paragraphs 24, 70, 85
Paste command 30, 37, 73, 79, 91, 100
Paste Special command 30, 79, 100, 101
Paste tool 37, 91
periods 86
Periods dialog box 86
PgDown key 75, 102
PgUp key 75, 102
Pick A Look Wizard 5, 86-89, 117, 136, 144
pictures. *See also* clip art; drawn objects; image formats
    adding to slides 90-91
    copying 91
    defined 6, 89
    moving 91
    removing 91
    resizing 91
pie charts 59, 60
placeholders 92
play lists 92
pointers 93
points 93
pop-up boxes 93
PowerPoint
    application window 2-3
    exiting 51
    starting 110-11
PowerPoint dialog box ... 5, 17, 110
PowerPoint Viewer application
    defined 9, 127
    installing 127, 148
    using 128
presentations
    active 13
    boilerplate structures for 16-18
    closing 30-31, 140
    color schemes for 32-34

presentations *(continued)*
    copying files 128-29
    creating 4-5
    defined 93
    dragging slides between 107
    erasing 50-51
    finding............................ 141-42
    moving from PC to Mac 15
    moving through slides 102
    naming 52, 98
    opening 80
    overview 4-5, 8-9
    printing 8, 94-95, 146
    renaming.................................. 99
    running (*see* slide shows)
    saving 31, 98-99, 140
    searching for 141-42
    spell-checking 108-9
    switching between 13
    title slide 84, 123
    troubleshooting layout 136-39
    unerasing 126
Presentation Template dialog box 117
Present It button 94
Print dialog box 94
printing
    black & white 144, 145
    canceling of 146-47
    to film recorder 12
    handouts 65
    presentations 8, 94-95, 146
    Speaker's Notes 76
    troubleshooting of 142-47
Print Manager 74, 95, 142, 143, 147
print spool................................. 147
Print tool 94
Program Manager...................... 127

Q

quitting PowerPoint 51

R

radar charts 59
recoloring clip art 29
  See also color schemes, changing
Recolor Picture dialog box 29
rectangles, drawing 43
Rectangle tool 43
rehearsing 95
removing. *See* deleting
renaming presentations 99
Replace dialog box 96
Replace Font dialog box 96
replacing
  bullets 24
  fonts 96
  text 96-97
Report It tool 52, 97
resizing
  clip art 28
  drawn objects 46
  objects 78, 91
  pictures 91
  text objects 121
  windows 35
Restore command 35
right aligning text 14
Rotate Left tool 46
Rotate Right tool 46
rulers 97
Run dialog box 127

S

saturation 98
Save As dialog box 98
Save tool 98, 99
saving
  color scheme changes 34
  presentations 31, 98-99, 140
Scale dialog box 78
scatter charts 60

scroll bars 48
Search dialog box 142
selecting
  data 99
  drawn objects 41
  OLE objects 99
  templates 117
selection cursor 100
Selection tool 42, 46
Send Backward tool 45
Shadow Color tool 44
Shadow On/Off tool 44
shadows
  adding 44, 77
  changing color 44, 77
shapes, freeform, drawing 43
sharing data between
  applications 6-7, 100-101
shortcut menus 101
Size command 35
Slide Background dialog box 103,
  145
slide buttons 102
Slide Color Scheme dialog
  box 32
Slide Masters
  adding objects 104
  adding slide numbers 104
  adding times and dates 104
  changing background color 22,
    103
  changing text formatting 103
  defined 102
  editing objects 104
  viewing 102
slide numbers 104
slides
  35mm 9, 12, 105
  annotating 14
  building 23
  changing background color 22,
    32, 34, 103
  choosing layout for 19-21
  defined 4, 105

slides *(continued)*
    dragging between
      presentations 107
    exporting 51-52
    hidden 66-67
    importing 69
    moving in Outline view 85
    moving through 102
    moving to Clipboard 74
    numbering 104
    setup for 12, 105
    titles for 107
    title slide 84, 123
    transition between 124-25
    troubleshooting layout 137
slides Setup dialog box 105
Slide Show dialog box 71, 106
slide shows. *See also* 35mm slides
    defined 8, 9
    looping 71
    play list 92
    rehearsing 95
    running with PowerPoint ... 106
    running with Viewer 9, 106-7
Slide Show view 71, 95, 106, 130
Slide Show View button 130
Slide Sorter View 107, 130
Slide Sorter View button 107, 130
Slide view 4, 19, 80, 102, 114, 130
Slide view button .. 80, 102, 114, 130
Snap to Grid command 64
sound, adding 108
spacing
    characters 26
    lines 70
Speaker's Notes
    creating 76
    defined 8, 108
    printing 76
    when to use 137
spell-checking presentations ...108-9
Spelling dialog box 108
Spelling tool 108

spreadsheets 112, 115, 137
squares, drawing 43
Standard toolbar 123, 160-61
starting PowerPoint 110-11
Summary Info dialog box 53
surface charts 60
switching tasks 36, 111-12
Switch To command ... 36, 74, 100,
    111-12
system resource memory 140

T

Tab key 116
Table AutoFormat command 116
tables
    adding as new slides 114
    adding to existing slides 112-13
    formatting 115-16
    as OLE objects 115-16
    and spreadsheets 112, 115
tabs 116
Task List dialog box 112
tasks, switching 111-12
templates
    color schemes 32-34
    defined 5, 116, 117
    finding 118
    selecting 117
text
    adding to slides in Outline
      view 119
    adding to slides in Slide
      view 120
    aligning 14
    anchoring in text objects 122
    ANSI characters 14-15, 121
    centering 14
    coloring 31
    copying 37, 121
    copying formatting 38
    deleting 40, 120

text *(continued)*
editing 48
ending lines 50
exporting 51-52
finding 54
formatting 38, 103
justifying 14
left aligning 14
moving 73, 121
replacing 96-97, 121
right aligning 14
Text Anchor dialog box 122
text boxes
adding 42
defined 118
vs. text objects 118
Text Color tool 31
text objects
adding to slides 119-20
aligning text within 14
anchoring text in 122
as bulleted items 24, 70, 85
copying text between 121
defined 76, 119
moving 121
moving text between 73, 121
in Outline view 119
paragraphs as 24, 70, 85
resizing 121
in Slide view 120
vs. text boxes 118
Text tool 42, 118
35mm slides 9, 12, 105
3-D charts 60
times, adding to slides 104
Tip of the Day 123
title bars 2
titles
for charts 61
for presentations 123
for slides 107
Titles dialog box 61
title slides 84, 123

toolbars
adding/removing 123
defined 3, 123-24
Formatting toolbar, list of
buttons 162
Graph toolbar, list of
buttons 165-66
Standard toolbar, list of
buttons 160-61
viewing button names 124
Tools Build command 23
Tools Hide Slide command ... 66, 67
Tools menu (Graph) 165
Tools menu (PowerPoint) 157
Tools Recolor command 29
Tools Replace Fonts command 96
Tools Spelling command 108
Tools Transition command 124
Tool Tips 124
traffic lights 139
transition between slides 124-25
Transition dialog box 124
troubleshooting
applications 148-49
files 140-42
Microsoft Windows 148-49
presentation layout 136-39
printing 142-47
slide layout 137
TrueType fonts 125

U

UNDELETE command
(MS-DOS) 126
Underline tool 126
Undo tool 126
unerasing presentation files 126
ungrouping
clip art 29
drawn objects 46
objects 104

Ungroup tool 46, 104
uppercase 25

V

vector images 126
    See also clip art
video, adding 127
Viewer application
    defined 9, 127
    installing 127, 148
    using 128
View Guides command 64
View Master command 102
View menu (Graph) 163
View menu (PowerPoint) 154
View Notes Pages command 76
View Outline command 82
View Ruler command 97
views
    defined 4, 129
    list of 130
    switching between 130
View Slide Show command 71,
    95, 106
View Slide Sorter command 107
View Toolbars command ... 42, 123
View Zoom command 134

W

Window menu (Graph) 165
Window menu
    (PowerPoint) 159-60
windows
    active vs. inactive 12-13
    application 12-13, 16
    closing 36
    Control-menu commands ... 35-36
    document 12-13, 40
    minimizing 35

windows *(continued)*
    moving 35
    resizing 35
    switching between 36
Windows environment 3, 148-49
Windows metafiles 51
wizards
    AutoContent 16-18
    defined 5, 130
    Pick A Look 5, 86-89, 117,
        136, 144
WordArt 130-33
wordwrapping 133
worksheets 112, 115, 137

X

xy (scatter) charts 60

Z

Zoom Control tool 134
zooming 134

The manuscript for this book was prepared and submitted to Microsoft Press in electronic form. Text files were prepared using Microsoft Word 6.0 for Windows. Pages were composed by Stephen L. Nelson, Inc., using PageMaker 5.0 for Windows, with text in Minion and display type in Copperplate. Composed pages were delivered to the printer as electronic prepress files.

COVER DESIGNER
Rebecca Geisler-Johnson

COVER ILLUSTRATOR
Eldon Doty

INTERIOR TEXT DESIGNER
The Understanding Business

PAGE LAYOUT AND TYPOGRAPHY
Stefan Knorr

COPY EDITOR
Pat Coleman

PROJECT EDITOR
Barbara Browne

TECHNICAL EDITOR
Barbara Browne

INDEXER
Julie Kawabata

Printed on recycled paper stock.